Resilience and Sustainability in Law

Resilience and Sustainability in Law:

Theoretical and Critical Approaches

By

Marco Ettore Grasso

Cambridge
Scholars
Publishing

Resilience and Sustainability in Law:
Theoretical and Critical Approaches

By Marco Ettore Grasso

This book first published 2021

Cambridge Scholars Publishing

Lady Stephenson Library, Newcastle upon Tyne, NE6 2PA, UK

British Library Cataloguing in Publication Data
A catalogue record for this book is available from the British Library

ISBN (10): 1-5275-7503-9
ISBN (13): 978-1-5275-7503-5

TABLE OF CONTENTS

SECTION 1

SUSTAINABILITY AND LAW

1. Introduction

The law in the field of sustainability has recently grown, alongside which open discussions about its qualification and its practical operations have emerged. Therefore, some theoretical approaches to sustainability will be described and critically examined. The functions of the law on the subject of sustainability are particularly important in this framework, as they concern solving potential conflicts among several types of norms. Theories concerning "weak" and "strong" views will be deepened through an analytical examination. The contrast between these ethics helps to shed light on a particular form of justice, which I have defined as "emergency sustainability".

2. Sustainable Development Law

In this section, I am going to describe the evolution of sustainable development law by undertaking an analytical examination of the main international sources.

Apart from the historical definition of sustainable development that is given in the Brundtland Report (1987)[1], the Rio Conference and more precisely Resolution n. 44/228 of December 21st 1989 (paragraph 15d) gave the assignment of promoting progressive development of "environmental international law" (see e.g., Bosselmann, 2020) and to verify the definition of the rights and duties of each State in the environmental field, in virtue of existing international legal measures[2]. The project of a binding code of rights and duties of nations was however put aside during the preparatory sessions and never carried out. It is likely the various countries feared the

---

[1] Sustainable development is development that meets the needs of the present, without compromising the ability of future generations to meet their own needs.

[2] General Assembly Resolution 44/228, 21 December 1989 (par. 15 d).

binding effects linked to norms concerning sustainable development (Grasso, 2015, 46). The International Court of Justice asserts that the principles of international law, among which is included also the principle of sustainable development, constituting the *ratio of* specific rules which do not satisfy criteria of *usus* and *opinio juris*[3], but rather determine standards of conduct, are intended to guide and homogenise the behaviours of several States.

As far back as 1996, the United Nations Commission on Sustainable Development filed a Report showing a series of principles on the subject of sustainability and underlined the role played by Agenda 21[4] and by the Declaration of Rio[5]. In 2002, the Committee on the juridical aspects of sustainable development, pertaining to the International Law Association, drafted the New Delhi Declaration on Principles of International Law relating to Sustainable Development. This declaration, despite being published as an official document of the United Nations (UN Doc A/57/329), does not have a binding force on the topic of sustainable development. The principles in question, furthermore, had already been declaimed by previous international sources, like the International Conference of Rio (1992) – more precisely the Charter of principles edited on the occasion of the same Conference – and Agenda 21. The principles taken into consideration by the New Delhi Declaration are, in fact, the principle of equity and abolishment of poverty; the principle of rational use and sustainability of natural resources; the principle of common but differentiated responsibilities; the principle of precaution; the principle of participation and of access to information and to justice in environmental matters; the principle of good administration; and the principle of integration. These principles are identified as a group of norms which make up an initial project in the emerging field of law and policies on sustainability (Schrijver, 2005). The Declaration seems to represent the point of arrival for a coherent and systematic elaboration of the principle of sustainable development within the legal sector. The New Delhi principles are influencing the decisions of dispute settlement bodies which have jurisdiction over many subjects[6]. Indeed, courts and tribunals are contributing to the

---

[3] "*Opinio juris*" concerns the conviction that a norm conforms to the law.

[4] United Nations Conference on Environment & Development, Rio de Janeiro, Brazil, 3 - 14 June 1992, Agenda 21. It is a non-binding action plan of the United Nations relating to sustainable development.

[5] United Nations Commission on Sustainable Development, 1995, Report of Principles of International Law for Sustainable Development, Geneva.

[6] Such as environmental issues, human rights, trade or investment.

world's Sustainable Development Goals[7]. Judges, in many jurisdictions, fight with the status of different environmental values as weighed against energy, economic, health and further national concerns (Gillroy, 2006, 42).

Also in 2002, ahead of the Johannesburg Summit, several judges at an international level adopted a document, "The Johannesburg Principles on the Role of Law and Sustainable Development". This document highlighted the need for assuring that environmental law and law in the field of sustainable development could greatly influence academic *curricula,* legal studies, and formation at all levels, in particular that of judges and other subjects involved in the jurisdictional process. This document showed also that in the framework of environmental law there is an urgent necessity to realise a work programme focalising on education, formation, and diffusion of information. In the same year, many jurists signed the mandate "International Jurists for the Implementation of International Sustainable Development Law", in which the same principles contained in the New Delhi Declaration were replicated[8], while in 2003 the Committee of International Law on Sustainable Development was founded. It is one among the twenty-four committees of the International Law Association, which has the task of studying the legal nature of this principle. Confirming the highly important role covered by the New Delhi Declaration, this Committee focalises its attention on the principle of integration, which seems without doubt to constitute a fundamental corollary of sustainable development. In this context, I want to highlight two reports written by this Committee: the first, in 2004, on the occasion of the Berlin Conference and the second, in 2006, during the Toronto Conference. If the first report praises the New Delhi Declaration, the second, instead, lays the accent on the principle of integration, considered the essential component of the concept of sustainability. Notwithstanding this, the nature of sustainable development does not seem at all clear.

The United Nations Conference on Sustainable Development "Rio + 20" (2012) ended with the adoption of Resolution n. 66/288 in which the

---

[7] The effectiveness of the Sustainable Development Goals can be discussed at length. In my own opinion, these goals are not always interconnected with each other within a defined conceptual framework.

[8] Namely, the principle of equity and the abolition of poverty; the principle of rational and sustainable use of natural resources; the principle of common but differentiated responsibilities; the precautionary principle; the principle of access to information, public participation, and access to justice in environmental matters; the principle of good administration; and the principle of integration.

conceptual and operative complexity of sustainable development is explained affirming that within this topic there are different approaches, visions, models and tools available to each country, under its national circumstances and priorities.

Under a constitutional profile, there are various Constitutions that take sustainable development into account. I would like to mention for example the Constitutions of Latin America, Africa and Asia, where such development plays an essential role in the State. In the Bolivian Constitution (2009)[9] "integral sustainable development" is mentioned in every part of the Constitution, and not merely in the titles related to habitat, rural development and resources, so much so that a class action against public authorities, individuals and groups who harm public health, the environment and natural patrimony has been configured. Asiatic Constitutions, moreover, evidence the link between sustainability and human right to environment. The Philippine Constitution (1987)[10], in turn, considers among its fundamental principles the duty of the State to safeguard personal rights to a healthy ecologically balanced environment as well as a right to good health. Such a duty is correlated in respect of the harmony of natural rhythms and development. The Constitution of Nepal (2015)[11], furthermore, declares the priority of environmental protection and the prevention of harm to development activities and takes on the commitment of favouring public awareness on environmental issues. The Indian Constitution (2019)[12] shows two basic elements of sustainable development too: the right of development, on the one hand, and on the other hand, the right to a healthy environment. From this point of view, even the Constitution of Kenya (2010)[13] is no less important, inasmuch as dimensions of equity emerge in respect to an equitable distribution of resources.

There is no doubt that environmental law is a fundamental component of sustainable development law. Therefore, before going on to describe

---

[9] The Constitution of Bolivia came into effect on February 7, 2009.

[10] The Constitution of the Philippines was ratified by a nationwide plebiscite on February 2, 1987.

[11] The Constitution of Nepal 2015 came into effect on September 20, 2015, replacing the Interim Constitution of 2007.

[12] The Constitution of India [as of 1st April, 2019] was brought into effect on 14.01.2019.

[13] The Constitution of Kenya was promulgated on 27 August 2010. The 2010 edition replaced the 1963 Independence Constitution.

some important theoretical aspects of sustainability law, I would like to describe the main characteristics of environmental law.

3. The Ethical Functions of Environmental Law

Before I start to describe the main functions of environmental law, let me start by saying that the environmental component (the relationship between man and the environment) is the best expression of sustainability. This is the reason why environmental law represents perhaps the most important matrix of sustainability ethics.

I will start by saying first of all that environmental law is a written and codified law, which is composed by several statutory rules: "secondary" or *competence* ones (which assign powers), "primary" rules (referring to behaviour), which might be described as "regulative rules", as they regulate behaviour and orient actions, and finally *constitutive* rules, which in a direct way constitute "*de facto status*", producing and realising certain situations or effects (for example let us only think about the environmental impact assessment procedure).

With regard to the distinctive features of environmental law, I would like to mention its *emergency* and *social* characteristics. Regarding the "emergency" aspect, environmental problems have often been faced according to their urgency, that is, after they have already produced catastrophic effects or effects serious enough to require immediate action. You can certainly notice a discrepancy between the political timelines and those characterising the environmental processes, with particular reference to the ones regarding degradation. The time horizon of policymakers, in fact, is unlikely to go beyond the next election date. The environmental legislation fully reflects this characteristic, with the presence of so called "hasty" rules. In addition to this, the unavailability of appropriate information concerning the causal relationship would lead policymakers to take decisions under conditions of high uncertainty, and this may constitute grounds for postponing these decisions.

The social character of this law, however, is outlined by an environmental justice seen as social justice, and recalls the need for a fair treatment for everyone, with the result that no population should bear an unfair portion of exposure to the effects of pollution and other environmental risks. This character, therefore, is inherent to the concept of distributive justice applied to natural resources, but also to the notions of "participation", as governed by the Aarhus Convention, and of "associations", developed with the contribution of the environmental movements.

The "sustainable soul" of environmental law is identified by its post-modern nature and "two-faced" character. This latter aspect highlights the contradictions inherent in environmental law, given that it, on the one hand, tends to pursue interests through a clear utilitarian connotation and, on the other hand, aims to protect the environment and its intrinsic value. However, these contradictions are not a symptom of the hypocrisy of this law, but rather they represent its effort to protect the natural world by also considering human needs, among which nonetheless some precise economic interests emerge.

Among the functions of this particular law, we recognise firstly a function of impulse for new public policies. The principles of this law are vital: the legislator adopts specific measures of implementation, foreseeing the consequent legislative adjustments. To cite an example: whenever within the European context there is uncertainty on the existence or extent of risk for human health, the principle of precaution allows the European community institutions to set up measures of safeguarding without necessarily having to wait for effectiveness or the seriousness of the risk level to become evident[14]. The principle of integration plays an important role in determining the most appropriate juridical bases for environmental measures. The encroachment of environmental law into the juridical sphere of some rights, for example property rights, can be justified principally by the impulse function in consideration.

The mentioned principles play an essential role even in the construction of the legal system, setting up a valid instrument aimed at a logical systematisation of the norms, and are characterised by values which complete the norms and determine their meaning. Such principles have the merit of identifying guidelines for the legislator, with the aim of qualifying norms within a unitary system and offering measures which are able to solve different cases homogeneously.

The systemic nature related to such principles enables environmental law to value itself critically each time. Nicolas De Sadeleer, instead of discussing "political principles" in regard to this, prefers to speak about "guiding principles", precisely to evidence the function of general orientation. Public authorities need more and more to be orientated and the

---

[14] Court of Justice of the European Communities, cause: C-157/96, 1998, 2265.

principles of environmental law guarantee such orientation, thus reconciling divergent interests. From this point of view, we can assume that this function of orientation is realised through a mediating activity, as the principles in question tend to balance various conflicting public interests. Whenever a public authority must decide whether to authorise a project which implies considerable impact on a protected natural area, national authorities should balance the imperative motives of relevant public interest, which represent the justification for the project, as well as the duty of avoiding any irreversible harm to biodiversity. When the European Commission is called upon to examine the various derogation requests concerning the legislation on competitiveness, the same Commission cannot derogate activities which would have harmful consequences on the environment. The European Court of Justice has established that under art.174 (2) of the European Treaty, communitarian policies regarding environmental matters must pursue the guarantee of a high level of safeguarding based on the principles of precaution and prevention[15].

The variety of institutional stakeholders operating in the field of environmental protection is without doubt considerable. Public policies on the environment concern the competences of many international, national and local operators. The guiding principles of environmental law are therefore subordinated to the interpretation of the numerous institutions which operate in this field. The nature of international environmental law is indeed particularly problematic, despite the efforts made in 1992 in Rio. It has proceeded in a fragmented way, never being "the product of any comprehensive or systematic scheme of law making, nor has it been based on any clearly defined pre-existing code of principles". European law, meanwhile, is affected by remarkable complexity and legislative articulation (Boyle, 1999).

These principles also have an operational function. The principle of precaution, for instance, through the implementation of measures of a prudential and cautionary nature, influences social actions and individual behaviours. In this regard, let us also remember the existence of the polluter pays principle, the principle of correction at source and the principle of prevention, which all push towards *ad personam* responsibility.

From the principles of environmental law, furthermore, we could extract an educational function, since they correspond to internationally fixed objectives in the field of environmental education. A synthesis of the

[15] Cause C-418/97 e C-419/97, 2000, in CGCE I-4512 (39).

principle evolutionary stages concerning this particular type of education should be drawn now.

During the Conference on the conservation of nature in Bangkok (1965), organised by the International Union for the conservation of nature, environmental education was directed towards the conservation of natural patrimony. In 1970, on the occasion of the conference promoted by the Union itself, environmental education was defined as a process of identification of values and concepts useful to develop the necessary attitudes and techniques for understanding existing interrelations between man, his culture and the biophysical environment surrounding him. During the United Nations Conference in Stockholm on the Environment (1972), the idea of eco-development was introduced. The necessity of regarding environmental problems as an integral part of economic development was underlined during this session. In this framework, environmental education detains the function of developing the link between environment and human activity. The Belgrade Charter (1975), on the other hand, is a predisposed document at inter-governmental level aimed at defining the objectives, principles and methods of environmental education. Later, in 1977, the Conference of Tbilisi organised by UNESCO and UNEP was held, where this education found a new collocation and promotion at regional and national levels in the scholastic curriculum at both preschool and post-university levels.

Successive developments then occurred in the years surrounding the turn of the millennium: during the United Nations Conference in Rio, environmental education was indicated as an essential element for the promotion of sustainable development; at the International Conference of Thessaloniki (1997), the conclusive Declaration on "*Environment and Society: education and awareness for sustainability*" was approved; and the United Nations Decade on education for sustainable development (2005) sought to deal with different environmental, social and economic implications. The aim of this decade is represented by the integration of the principles, values and practices of sustainable development in all aspects of education and learning. Similarly, in UNECE Strategy, aimed at promoting education in favour of sustainable development (Vilnius, 2005), such education is defined as a permanent process which interests the individual throughout their entire life span. It is not limited to formal learning, but is extended also to informal learning. Education is a human right as well as a pre-requisite for good governance, for informed decision-making, and for the promotion of democracy. Even in the international workshop held in Belgrade in 2005, environmental education was qualified as an element directed towards the construction of a new universal ethics, capable of emphasising individual and social behaviours compatible with the place that humanity occupies in the biosphere and capable of reacting with sensitivity to the complex and ever-changing relationship between nature and humanity. An equally significant role is attributable to the World Conference on Education for Sustainable Development (Bonn, 2009) that incorporates the results gained in the above-mentioned Decade and sets the stage for future strategies to be carried out. In the light of this synthetic chronology related to the principal stages on environmental education, we realise that the fundamental values, which are the basis for this education, correspond fundamentally to the objectives that the principles of environmental law intend to pursue. It is therefore possible to discuss in favour of an educative function of this right, exercised through its principles that, moreover, may be qualified as rules of conduct, since they prescribe the behaviours to be followed.

4. The Nature(s) of Environmental Law

The post-modern nature of environmental law includes a profile that might be described as fragile and complex, functional to the concept of risk and environmental guidelines. We must say that one of the main elements characterising post-modernity is given by the presence of *guiding principles* aimed at balancing different interests. These principles represent in the sector of the constituent law the best example of discipline oriented to goals, which then describes the legal area mainly characterised by post-modern elements[16]. The environmental law principles seem to mark in a particularly clear way the transition from modern law to post-modern law, marked by the pragmatic nature of rules. They are required by specific legislation and are therefore likely to be applied directly by the public authorities, although often the more political nature is more emphasised than the strictly legal one (Grasso, 2015).

There is no doubt, in any case, that the principles in question carry out different functions, for both social and legal significance. The scientific literature on environmental law principles is certainly considerable. Both European studies and those outside of Europe, in fact, have examined them in detail and individually studied them in-depth under a legal and political profile. Only at European level according to Art. 174 of the Treaty, the Community policy on the environment is based on the precautionary

---

[16] The contemporary law is in effect a law structured for targets.

principles and preventive action, on the principle of priority correction at the source of the environmental damage and on the 'polluter pays' principle. Keep in mind that the principles of environmental law can be considered true conceptual corollaries of the "sustainable norm" and therefore of sustainable law. The principles of prevention, integration and precaution, for example, can build bridges between regulatory areas that have little interest or conflict between them. Consequently, these principles can become new interpretive tools to resolve disputes arising in different areas of international law (such as the conflict between multilateral environmental Agreements and WTO obligations). We must, however, point out that such principles can eliminate the points of conflict, but not necessarily solve them in a definitive manner; therefore, the importance of greater integration of environmental interests within commercial legal systems (such as those of the WTO and of the EC internal market) is really opportune.

In the post-modern perspective, environmental law will no doubt be recognised thanks to a certain *fragility*. This right, in fact, by its very nature is often in conflict with the interests and rights coming from the economic and commercial sphere. The right on economic issues certainly represents the strongest right, the one that embodies the interests and demands for which, often, strong powers are indeed hidden, while the environmental law defending the environment in the strict sense or a human's needs through the environment, is in a distinct disadvantage.

To resolve the conflictual relationship between environmental law and economic law, the representatives of the European Community and the Member States adopted in Marrakesh (1994) a direct decision to coordinate trade and environmental policies within the limits of the competence of the multilateral trading system[17]. The Decision requires the establishment of a committee that can propose changes to this system, in order to improve the interaction between trade and environment and to avoid protectionist trade measures, thereby ensuring the pursuit of the environmental aims of Agenda 21 and of the Declaration of Rio. It also ensures the monitoring of trade measures with environmental purposes, as well as environmental measures identified by commercial profiles, thereby allowing the implementation of the multilateral disciplines that govern such measures.

---

[17] Communication of the Committee of the GATT trade negotiations, *Decision on Trade and Environment*, GATT Doc. MTN.TNC/W/141, 29 March 1994.

Despite some decisions of this Organization, such as *Gasoline*[18] *and Shrimp/Turtle* (2002)[19], we have recognised that even in the case of multilateral trade measures, the WTO system is not a regime tightly closed so as to refuse to consider principles of environmental law; from the global point of view, the environmental measures related to trade are often in conflict with the WTO agreement. Similarly, at the European level, the use by Member States of trade restrictions for environmental purposes would be in contrast with the principle of free movement of goods.

The aforementioned fragility is also apparent given that the examined law, more than any other, is often confronted with the "risk" variable. Most of the provisions on the environment, in fact, consider the risk within their structure. In other words, we could easily recognise the risk of a peculiar trait of environmental law, so that it can be identified as a "friend-enemy" of the same law. If friendship was justified by the strong link between the two variables, the enmity instead would be explained by the fact that the risk is often configured as an obstacle to the same environmental guidelines, sometimes constituting the grounds for the postponement of political and administrative decisions. The precautionary principle, for example, considers the fundamental concept of risk. Some political decisions result in significant effects on the environment, not all predictable, that could represent a harm to the society in general or specific persons in particular; therefore, the menace of the environment can be represented as the result of decisions and is interpreted according to the risk category.

Within the post-modern nature of environmental law, we also find its character represented by *complexity*, mainly caused by the continuing and growing need for legislative intervention, as well as the difficulty of equitably balancing the different interdisciplinary skills. This law, in fact, is characterised by the theoretical difficulty of ensuring unity in legislation affecting contexts and purposes inconsistent with each other. This difficulty can in large part be explained with the traditional separation between legal science and the natural sciences. The practical nature of the law indeed led jurists to dissociate the different constituent elements of ecosystems and to

---

[18] In this case, the WTO Appellate Body stated that "customary rules of interpretation" would include art. 31 of the Vienna Convention of 1996, which "has attained the status of a rule of customary or general International law" (Gasoline: 17).

[19] According to the WTO Appellate Body, the concept of "natural exhaustible resources" must be interpreted "in the light of contemporary concerns of the community of nations about the protection and conservation of the environment" (Appellate Body, Shrimp, par. 129).

acquire them in accordance with their immediate economic value. Environmental law is an interdisciplinary science that incorporates knowledge from the different nature of the law and has a strong technical matrix. It is not always the legislator who decides the sense of the norm, but rather those who impose parameters and limits and who would have the ambition to dictate the rules of conduct governing the different cases.

From another viewpoint, the nature of environmental law on the one hand corresponds to a view of environmental protection, instrumental to the satisfaction of human needs, which sees the human being as the direct recipient of environmental law; on the other hand, instead, the nature of this law is represented by the protection of the environment as it is. That is to say, as an entity with its own value and capable of being the direct beneficiary of the laws.

If the first aspect of its nature has led towards the recognition of rights that relate to the environmental sphere and interprets the damage to the environment through anthropocentric parameters, such as the financial loss suffered as a result of damage, the second aspect of its nature has opened the way to the "rights of nature" and assesses environmental damage through forms of *restitutio in integrum,* aimed at returning the value to the damaged environment.

The "two-faced" character of environmental law highlights its inherent contradictions, summarised in the conflict between utilitarian interests and interests aimed at the intrinsic good of the environment itself. The conflictual link between the extrinsic value and the intrinsic value of natural goods translates within the sphere of law in the link – not always consistent – between the rights of nature and human, social, and economic rights.

Similarly, the connection between a "weak approach" to sustainability and a utilitarian side of environmental law, as well as the connection between the "strong approach" to sustainability and the ecological side of this law, is particularly evident within this framework. In effect, the two-faced nature of environmental law finds a perfect and logical correspondence in the existing bipartition in the field of sustainability: "strong" and "weak" approaches. In other words, the utilitarian side of environmental law corresponds to a weak approach applied to environmental sustainability. Conversely, the side linked to the rights of nature is connected instead to a strong approach to this sustainability.

Even qualifying the right to the environment as the "right to human life" or "right to a healthy environment" would clearly fall into the conceptual sphere of a weak vision (utilitarian), because the protection of environment would be instrumental compared to human life and human health. A similar consideration could be made if we decided to protect the environment only in view of our existence and future generations, that is, in accordance with an instrumental key.

Nevertheless, I think that we cannot speak of anthropocentrism or utilitarianism, or even more of a weak approach, to the extent that we want to guarantee a healthy living environment for us and for the generations to come or if we want to qualify the environmental right as a right to life. Our natural environment in fact is our "common home". Therefore, I will be describing these two particular meanings of environmental law in the next two sections, taking this premise into account.

4.1. Environmental Law as Right to Human Life

The Aarhus Convention on the access to information, the public participation in decision-making, and the access to justice in environmental matters (1998) recognises that an adequate protection of the environment is essential to human well-being, given that every human has the right to live in an environment capable of ensuring the protection of their health and well-being as well as the individual and the collective duty to protect and enhance the environment in the interest of present and future generations.

In this regard, in the lawsuit Joseph D. Kessy *vs*. the City Council of Dar es Salaam[20] (1998) the residents of Tabata, a suburb of Dar es Salaam, Tanzania, made an application to the Supreme Court to obtain an injunction to ensure that the City Council desisted from continuing to dump garbage in that area. This Council, on the contrary, asked to be allowed to continue their activities. The Court, denying the Council this request, believed that activity would endanger the health and lives of the appellant, thus violating the constitutional right to life[21].

[20] Supreme Court of Tanzania, civil case 29/1998.

[21] In other words the judge Lugakingira wrote: "I have never heard it anywhere before for a public authority, or even an individual to go to court and confidently seek for permission to pollute the environment and endanger people's lives, regardless of their number. Such wonders appear to be peculiarly Tanzanian, but I regret to say that it is not given to any court to grant such a prayer. Article 14 of our

The lawsuit submitted to the Supreme Court of Sri Lanka, *Deshan Harinda (a minor) et al. vs. Ceylon Electricity Board et al.* (also known as the case "Kotte Kids", 1998)[22] is also significant, where a group of children promoted a legal proceeding in which they stated that the noise from a power plant exceeded the allowable noise level, causing – amongst other things – hearing loss. Although the Constitution of Sri Lanka did not expressly impose the right to life, it was argued that all other constitutionally enshrined rights necessarily presupposed the existence of this right.

In the lawsuit *Subash Kumar vs. State of Bihar*[23] (1991), the applicants complained about the violation of the right to life, compromised because of the pollution of the River Bokaro, caused by the wastewaters from the Tata Iron Steel Company. The Court recognised that this right includes the right to the enjoyment of unpolluted water and air, setting that in face of any risk relating to the quality of life, any concerned person can assert action aiming to claim the fundamental rights of the community or of a group which is not able to assert their rights for failure, poverty or ignorance of the law.

Even in the lawsuit of the Pakistani *Shehla Zia and Others vs. WAPDA* (1994)[24], a case concerning electromagnetic pollution matters, the right to life is qualified as environmental law and as healthy environment law in particular. The judge in this case clearly expressed that life cannot be limited to mere existence, understood as a time lag between conception and death.

Furthermore, we quote herewith the lawsuit *Lalanath de Silva vs. The Minister of Forestry and Environment*[25] (1998), where the applicants complained that the Ministry of Environment had predisposed air quality standards, which were clearly contrary to the right to life. Therefore, the Supreme Court ordered the enactment of regulations aimed to control the air pollution caused by vehicle emissions in the city of Colombo.

The human right to the environment is a precondition for defining further rights. Under the comparative profile, it is worth recalling some

---

constitution provides that every person has a right to live and to protection of his life by the society. It is therefore, a contradiction in terms and a denial of this basic right deliberately to expose anybody's life to danger or, what is eminently monstrous, to enlist the assistance of the court in this infringement."

[22] Kotte Kids case (1998).

[23] Subhash Kumar *vs*. Bihar et al., A.I.R. 1991 S.C. 420 (1991) (India).

[24] Ms. Shehla Zia et al. *vs*. WAPDA, P.L.D. 1994 S.C. 693.

[25] Supreme Court of Sri Lanka, Lalanath de Silva *vs*. Minister of Forestry & Env. (The Air Pollution Case), 1998.

constitutional provisions that create a secure anthropocentric view of environmental law. Article 45 of the Spanish Constitution (October 31, 1978), for example, establishes the right of everyone to an adequate environment. Article 66 of the Portuguese Constitution (dated April 2, 1976) mentions the right to a humane, healthy and ecologically balanced environment. Article 101 of the National Environmental Policy of the United States Act (1969) also recognises the right to a healthy environment. Other Constitutions consider the right to a balanced environment too (Peru and Thailand) whereas others, instead, prefer to argue about the value of the environment through the protection of natural resources (for example, the constitutions of Canada and China). The right to the environment as the right to human life is clearly present in the Constitution of Ecuador (2009), which sees Mother Earth (*Pachamama*) as a subject of law. In fact, the intention of creating a "new form of citizen coexistence in harmony with nature" has been declared in order to pursue the "*buen vivir*", the "*sumak kawsay*". The Ecuadorian Constitution enshrines the rights of this "*vivir*", pertaining to a healthy environment, health, water, food, housing, culture, information, communication, education, science and business. The "*buen vivir*" includes both rules relating to inclusion/social equality and rules relating to biodiversity and more generally to natural resources. In the Bolivian Constitution, however, good living is a concept of a collective and communitarian matrix that manages to complete individual interest.

4.2. Environmental Law as Right to a Healthy Environment

The right to human life finds its best form of expression in the "right to a healthy environment". In this regard, the General Assembly of the United Nations confirmed the existence of a right to the environment in its 1990 Resolution. It welcomed the decision of the Commission on Human Rights and of the Sub-Commission on Minorities to study the relationship between human rights and the environment, observing that all individuals are entitled to live in an environment which is adequate for their health and their well-being[26]. Although that resolution confirmed the relationship between environmental degradation and human rights, this was still far away from the recognition of the right to a healthy environment. Articles on human rights and the environment adopted by the Sub-Commission on Minorities, in fact, had no resonance. The "Experts' Sustainable Development Report" also noted that the right to a healthy environment constituted an instrument

[26] United Nations General Assembly Resolution 45/94, UN GAOR, 45° session, UN Doc. A/RES/45/94 (1991).

to integrate the environmental sphere with that of development. In this sense, the sustainability of development would seem subjected to the condition that the right to a healthy environment is realised. The Stockholm Declaration (1972) already affirmed the human right to a healthy and dignified life. In Art. 1 of the Rio de Janeiro Declaration, we can also read that human beings are entitled to a healthy and productive life in harmony with nature. Principle 14 of the same Declaration also recalled the importance of monitoring any activity or substance that is considered harmful to human health.

The European Court of Human Rights in Strasbourg, however, drew up a precise notion of the right to the environment by relating it to the protection of the right to health. The lawsuits *López-Ostra vs. Spain* (1994)[27] and *Guerra vs. Italy* (1998) are examples of this: in the case law of this Court, in fact, the effort to grant a more extensive protection to the environmental dimension of human health emerged. Even Judge Weeramantry, of the International Court of Justice, in his dissenting opinion expressed on September 25, 1997 in connection with the lawsuit *Gabčíkovo vs. Nagymaros*[28] stated that environmental protection is a vital part of the theory of human rights, necessarily integrated with the right to health and more generally with the right to life.

Even the World Health Organization (WHO) has stated on numerous occasions that the right to health is related to environmental injuries. In 1976 the Executive Body of the WHO recommended that the World Health Assembly adopt a resolution directed to governments in order to make environmental health programmes an integral part of national health policy and development strategies[29]. The resolution adopted by this Assembly on January 27, 1976 considered that the improvement of environmental conditions should be seen as part of the efforts to promote development and health protection. In 1989, the Executive Body of the WHO reported that the environmental degradation caused by the indiscriminate use of technology constitutes a threat to human health; hence, a new World Health Assembly resolution directed to the Member States to evaluate policies and strategies aimed at preventing the adverse effects of development on the environment and on human health. The international community is

---

[27] European Court of Human Rights, López-Ostra *vs*. Spain, Series A, No. 303 C, 1994; European Court of Human Rights, Guerra et al. *vs*. Italia, Case 14967/89, 1998.

[28] International Court of Justice, Gabčíkovo *vs*. Nagymaros, 1997.

[29] WHO EB57.R28 Resolution, Geneva, 1976.

frequently called upon to strengthen its support for activities that promote a healthy environment and to monitor the adverse effects of development on the environment and human health[30]. The Stockholm Convention on Persistent Organic Pollutants, for example, aims to protect human health and the environment. Similarly, the Protocol on Water and Health (London, 1999), borne out of the Convention on the Protection and Use of Transboundary Watercourses and International Lakes (Helsinki, 1992), is aimed to promote the protection of human health and welfare at all levels in accordance with both an individual and a collective point of view. The UN Committee on Economic and Social Rights, moreover, believed that the right to the highest viable level of physical and mental health, contained in Article. 12.1 of the Covenant on Economic, Social and Cultural Rights, was not to be limited to the right to health in the strict sense: the right to health, in fact, carries over into other rights, like the right to potable water and the right to a healthy environment. Even the American Declaration of the Rights and Duties of Man (1948) establishes that every man has the right to preserve his health through sanitary and social measures related to food, clothing, housing and medical care. This guarantee is interpreted in the Protocol at the American Convention on Human Rights in the area of economic, social and cultural rights (art. 10 of the San Salvador Protocol) as a chance to ensure the enjoyment of the highest possible standard of physical, mental and social welfare. The right to health protection, as mentioned in the American Declaration, necessarily includes a prohibition of environmental degradation because otherwise health would be damaged.

The right to a healthy environment is well established as part of the rights of indigenous people. The Inter-American Court for Human Rights, in relation to the *Awas Tingni* case (2001), considered that the lack of prevention of environmental damage on indigenous lands brought prejudices to the same indigenous people since the possibility of maintaining a social unit depends on its collective and communitarian existence as well as on the maintenance of the land. Similarly, in the decision of the *Belize Maya* case (2004), the Inter-American Commission on Human Rights claimed that the rights violation of the Mayan people had been exacerbated by the environmental damage done to their lands. Previously, in its Report on the situation of human rights in Ecuador on April 24, 1997, the Commission had already reported that "Indigenous peoples maintain special ties with their traditional lands, and a close

---

[30] WHO EB83.R15 Resolution, Geneva, 1989.

dependence upon the natural resources provided therein – respect for which is essential to their physical and cultural survival".

In the case concerning the Yanomami Indians, on March 5, 1985, the Inter-American Commission on Human Rights again recalled that the damage to people resulting from environmental degradation violates the right to health in Art. XI of the American Declaration.

The need to protect the quality of the environment (and thus the guarantee of a healthy environment) is globally recognised as an essential component of indigenous culture, from the Brundtland Report of 1987 and principle 22 of the Declaration on Environment and Development of 1992, to the Convention on Biological Diversity of 1992 and the Declaration on the Establishment of the Arctic Council. When the conditions that sustain the traditional culture of indigenous peoples are missing, the settlement of the inhabitants in other areas will inevitably lead to the elimination of the culture of these peoples and thus to the loss of their identity[31].

---

[31] In the *Saramaka People vs. Suriname* case (2007), for instance, the serious environmental degradation resulting from the abuse of the Saramaka, a population descending from the Maroons (slaves of African origin), was seriously lamented. The Centre for Minority Rights Development (Kenya) and Minority Rights Group International on Behalf of Endorois Welfare Council *vs*. Kenya case (2010) concerns the forced relocation of Endorois communities from their ancestral lands and their denial of access to the same lands and to its traditional resources, because of a mining concession.
The heavy exploitation of indigenous lands is also well exemplified in the experience of the ethnic groups of the Maasai and Ogiek in Kenya. The Mau Forest is located on the western side of the high plain of the Rift Valley and is the largest complex system of forests and waterways in Kenya. Before the British colonisation, which took place in the early 1900s, groups of the Maasai and the Ogiek lived in the areas nearby. The British, after colonising these territories, began to build a railway network, forcefully deforesting the area, in order to recover spaces and use wood as fuel. In addition to the deforestation, the expulsion of ethnic inhabitants and the destruction of different native species and natural ecosystems occurred. The traditional knowledge of these ethnic groups was supplanted by industrial activities linked to deforestation by settlers, who took possession of the forest and the management of its resources. Later, the British government established a new system aimed at the cultivation of deforested areas for the three years following deforestation, and from the fourth year the portions of cultivated land would have been affected by the operations of reforestation. This system was named the *Shamba System*. The reforestation and the cultivation, however, did not take account either of the native species or traditional knowledge of the Maasai and Ogiek. Indeed,

Let us remember that the Supreme Court of Nepal in the lawsuit *Suray Prasad Sharma Dhungel vs. Godavari Marble Industries et al.* (1995)[32] deemed that a healthy environment was part of the constitutional right to life. Similarly, the Supreme Court of Kenya in the lawsuit *Waweru vs. Republic* (2006)[33] deemed that the constitutional right to life, as established in Section 71 of the Constitution of Kenya, had to grant the right to a clean and healthy environment. More precisely, the Court stated that all people "are entitled to the right to life – In our view the right to life is not just a matter of keeping body and soul together because in this modern age that right could be threatened by many things including the environment".

In the lawsuit *Sharma et al. vs. Nepal Drinking Water Corporation et al.* (2001), the Supreme Court noted the exclusive role of drinking water compared to public health, stating that its decision could be a valid example of responsibility for a welfare state[34].

Parallel to the right to a healthy environment law, we have the right that arises in connection with disturbances and environmental interferences that the common law legal system defines as *environmental nuisances*.

5. Qualifications of the Concept of "Sustainable Development Law"

Legal-political theories on sustainability are affected by the theoretical bipartition between "weak" and "strong" approaches. The former see

---

European crops considered most profitable for the timber market were planted. The change of species also brought about a change in power and the traditional culture of the local people. Only in the sixties did Kenya gain independence from the United Kingdom. Nevertheless, only the richest and the most influential of the population were able to achieve benefits from independence. The new Vice President of Kenya, in fact, abolished the *Shamba System*, implementing a new management system of the forest that originally provided for the restoration and redistribution of areas of lands to indigenous communities. Subsequently, on the contrary, due to high levels of corruption, the forest was divided and assigned to the new President and to the most influential people of the Molo district: only 10% of the territory was attributed to the Ogiek. The privatisation of forests led to the signing of short-term contracts relating to the granting of forest portions. Deforestation in these areas has already had harmful effects, causing ecological disasters of large dimensions that in the near future may even cause global catastrophes.

[32] Supreme Court of Nepal, Dhungel *vs*. Godavari Marble Indus., No. 35, 1995.

[33] Waweru *vs.* Republic, 1 K.L.R. 677-700 (H.C.K), Kenya, 2006.

[34] Supreme Court of Nepal, Sharma *vs*. Nepal Drinking Water Corp., No. 2237, 2001.

sustainability as an interaction between different spheres (including the ecological sphere) and are distinguished by a non-ecocentric integrative nature. The latter instead are characterised by a clearly ecocentric matrix. Therefore, even the opinions of sustainability law scholars have divided substantially between those who highlight the integrative dimension and those who highlight the pre-eminent ecological role.

There is no single definition attributable to sustainable development law. Rather, different theoretical qualifications can be attributed to this particular law. In general terms, law experts were mostly worried about interpreting the concept of sustainable development[35] through the identification of a group of legal principles, which would be able to solve the conflict between rules related to economic law, law concerning social development, and also to environmental law. In this way, sustainable development could even be considered a meta-principle of procedural character inclined to influence the decisions of international courts.

The nature of the principle of sustainable development does not seem at all peaceful. Its condition is strictly correlated to its definition. Vaughn Lowe, in these terms, has observed that the vagueness of the concept is incompatible with it having a "norm-creating character" (Lowe, 1999). Sustainable development would indeed be an "umbrella term", that is an inclusive concept, capable of holding within itself different shades of meaning, including both substantial and procedural components. According to Lowe's theory, it is a "meta-principle" capable of exercising an "interstitial normativity", compared to further legal norms, whenever the latter conflict with each other or overlap[36]. Lowe adopts the notion of "modifying norms", that is norms that have the function of modifying the efficiency of primary norms and which do not depend on their own juridical condition, but which can be applied directly by Courts. In this sense, sustainable development is therefore a "modifying norm" which reconciles development with protection of the environment. If Lowe considers that the vagueness of the concept lies mainly in the way of pursuing the juridical condition, Hunter *et alias*, instead, argue that the very same concept has been accepted by different States in virtue of its ambiguity (Hunter, Salzman

---

[35] In the history of the concept of sustainable development, two schools of thought have been identified. They refer to the 'weak' and 'strong' interpretations of this concept.

[36] The different dimensions of sustainability help to identify the concept of sustainable development as a "variegated" concept, not tethered to one conceptual mooring.

and Zaelke, 2007). If, on the one hand, such peculiar development is more than just a simple concept, as the States invoke it relatively to their own development activities, on the other hand, it seems to be lacking in any certain and substantial normative quality. Ellis and Wood also speak about a meta-principle of environmental law (Ellis and Wood 2006) and Wilkinson describes it as a meta-principle in reference to which the other principles, which develop its content, are identified (Wilkinson, 2002).

As noted by Cordonier Segger and Khalfan, sustainable development is a norm detaining the function of balancing conflicting juridical norms, concerning precisely socioeconomic development and the safeguarding of the environment (Cordonier Segger and Khalfan, 2004).

For Birnie and Boyle, some doubts exist about the nature of the development that I am discussing. They wonder whether it should be considered a form of domestic policy, which influences decisional processes at national level, or rather a principle that tries to influence the behaviour of States on an international level (Birnie and Boyle, 1994). The answer lies in the observation that sustainable development is characterised by both natures as it is an international principle, which attempts to impact decisional processes at a national level.

The prominent academic John Dernbach believes that the effective meaning of the concept under discussion must be sought above all in Agenda 21, in the Declaration of Rio, and in other national political documents, and that such a concept should furnish a range of useful instruments to strengthen governance. Dernbach also identifies unsolved issues within the area of sustainability, such as the responsibility of developed countries and developing countries and the role of international commerce (Dernbach, 2002). Sands, for his part, claims that "there can be little doubt that the concept of sustainable development has entered the corpus of International customary law, requiring different streams of international law to be treated in an integrated manner" (Sands, 2003, 208). The condition of such development can be seen in the juridical dimension, which refers to processes, principles and objectives, as well as a large corpus of international agreements connected with the environment on economic, civil and political rights (Sands, 1994): its legal status thus seems to be approximately between a norm and a concept. It requires the application of the existing principles, norms and institutional apparatus in an integrated style. Segger, on the contrary, evincing doubts on the legal nature of the concept, maintains that it is not indisputable to consider that this form of development represents a principle of customary law of the environment (Cordonier Segger and Weeramantry, 2005).

According to Bosselmann, who promotes a strong vision by "ecological law", sustainability instead should be seen as a recognised legal principle, which could be applied to the entire legal system, rather than just environmental law, regardless of its international or domestic levels (Bosselmann, 2008).

In my opinion, sustainability law is based on a meta-legal, holistic and moral nature, and it is recognisable as a customary norm with a strictly interdisciplinary character. Sustainable responsibility, then, consists of several elements and is mainly embodied in value-based, common, equitable and intergenerational responsibilities, where ample space is given to virtues and integrity (moral and ecological). It goes beyond a merely 'weak' approach, so too a 'strong' one of sustainable development, and is placed within a "balanced sustainability", which lies between an ecocentric (not extremist) vision and one of "responsible anthropocentrism" (Grasso, 2015). My vision of sustainability is confronted with environmental and health emergencies: it is mainly linked to catastrophic emergencies, such as those connected to extreme events, so much so that I recently theorised a new branch of sustainability: "Emergency Sustainability" (Grasso 2019).

6. Some Theoretical Issues about the "Open" Dimensions of Sustainability Law

Sustainable development presupposes that infinite economic growth on the planet is impossible (Georgescu-Roegen 1986). "Sustainable law" or law on the subject of sustainability should necessarily be read with a "global"[37] key (Kelsen, 1967), or at least should be as open as possible, so as to include several interactions among various knowledge systems. In 1997 Günther Teubner was speaking of a "Global Bukowina" (a phrase first used by Ehrlich, 1936)[38]. According to Teubner, in fact, global law can only be explained by a theory of legal pluralism turning from the law of colonial

[37] In this sense, for example, a "global law" could be justified through the legal philosophical Kelsenian theories of purity and normative unity of law, which seem to link several governance reasons within a greater system of law.

[38] Eugen Ehrlich (1936) spoke first regarding a "Global Bukowina". According to him, it is civil society that will globalise its legal orders.

societies to the laws of several ethnic, religious and cultural communities in modern States (Teubner, 1997).

The intersections of legal systems of different natures were theorised by André-Jean Arnaud (Arnaud, 1981). The inter-legality – or rather the simultaneous insertion of every single subject or group of subjects within a series of distinct normative systems in virtue of the nature of single acts or single expectations – was emphasised by Boaventura de Sousa Santos in his *Toward a New Common Sense* (De Sousa Santos, 1995). Last but not least, the essay by François Ost and Michel Van De Kerchove on the passage from the "pyramid" to a "network" is worthy of mention (Ost and Van De Kerchove, 2002).

Most environmental problems are not contained within State boundaries, but affect the biosphere and are therefore inherently global concerns (Gillroy, 2006). According to Twining, furthermore, a healthy cosmopolitan discipline of law should encompass all levels of social relations (Twining, 2009). He explores the implications of adopting a global, or rather, a "general" perspective for a number of particular topics, such as diffusion of law[39] and the relationship between law and development. The concept of "general jurisprudence" should be interpreted broadly to include any general enquiries about law that go beyond legal cultures (Twining, 2009). In this sense, law can be viewed as a "heritage", an "ideology", or even the activity of "theorising". It is precisely in this last sense that this work sees the role and function of "law in action"[40] on sustainable development, namely as a possibility of theorisation. In the following section, I will outline the theories on the functions of law in order to discuss in particular the ethical functions of sustainability law, which relate mainly to the reduction of complexity and to the solution of potential conflicts between conflicting norms.

7. The Functions of Law: Theoretical Aspects

In order to describe the functions of sustainability law, a short theoretical analysis concerning the general branch of the functions of law should be

---

[39] Chapter 9 considers critically some assumptions about the literature on "reception" and "transplantation" of law and offers a new framework for the study of diffusion.
[40] "Law in action" is a legal theory examining the role of law as a tool connected to society. The first reference may have been a 1910 paper by Roscoe Pound, that was a forerunner to the legal realism movement.

considered. Therefore, a few considerations about the philosophical-juridical theory on this topic will be dealt with.

The position of Niklas Luhmann seems crucial at this juncture, among the different critical reconstructions. In his opinion, law has the function of reducing complexity and stabilising contingency, making a choice among possible incompatible expectations, on the basis of normative reference points, thereby bringing about a decrease in the degree of incertitude which is in principle characterising human action. According to the German scholar, the human environment has in fact moved by a multitude of subjective expectations, which are much greater than the possibility to satisfy them, and is marked by great incertitude and a high degree of contingency of actions and events (Luhmann, 1981); that is, a world where actions and events are theoretically possible and equally probable. The game of subjective expectations is represented by Luhmann as a game of reflexive mirrors, where a subject acts not only in relation to the expectations of another, but rather in relation to the expectations that another nurtures towards him and so on to infinity. Therefore, this over-complex environment needs to be simplified. Hence, human action is organised through social systems that Luhmann considers to be self-constituted communicative structures, gifted with sense, possessing the aim of reducing complexity and allowing choice within incompatible alternatives.

Under a theoretical profile, social complexity, interpreted as a surplus of theoretical possibilities of action compared to actual experimental ones, can be reduced by selecting some possibilities among the eligible ones. It is here that power reveals itself, just like a reductive instrument, by definition, as it consists in the possibility of selecting by its own decision an alternative for others and in reducing social complexity. Social systems, characterised by communicative actions, play the role of attributing a shared social sense towards actions and offer useful criteria for choosing among the numerous possible alternatives of action put forward by the environment, which is extremely complex and contingent. Therefore, social action coincides with communication through socially shared sense schemes. Moreover, the systems of social communication do not live apart from others but rather together with interaction systems, which involve individuals and interact through structural couplings, namely "*strukturelle kopplung*", allowing them to transfer meaning to each other (Luhmann, 1984). Describing these couplings, Luhmann indicates a method of reconciliation of intra-systemic self-referentiality and inter-systemic exchanges, two concepts in apparent contradiction. He defines the structural couplings as forms of simultaneous relationships, strategic co-ordinations. In other words, the theory of autopoietic systems substitutes the traditional input/output model with the concept of structural couplings. Through such couplings, a system can be connected to highly complex environmental systems. In the absence of these couplings in social sub-systems relations, the law is considered “corrupt”. Events that are connected can cause structural modifications within the system, which consist in mere autopoietic operations, through which the systems reconstruct themselves, adding and eliminating elements in favour of new functional needs (Luhmann, 1993).

According to Luhmann, the law originates from social expectations and in particular, from normative expectations that individuals still hold when they are disregarded. It is a social sub-system, structurally made up of social communications, normatively orientated, and functionally aimed at reducing complexity. This happens thanks to its ability to render normative expectations congruent, allowing for decisions among incompatible expectations. This sub-system is self-referential, like other social sub-systems. At the same time, the law presents characters of units (*Einheit*) and closure (*Geschlossenheit*), towards the external environment. It is autopoietic because it constitutes its own fundamental elements and acts according to a logic, which corresponds to the “licit-illicit” binary code (*Recht-Unrecht*). The acts of normative communication of which the legal system is composed detain a meaning on the basis of logical-semantic links, which can be found within the juridical system and are determined through an auto-reproductive process. Therefore, despite the fact that the legal system receives input from the external environment, from an operative point of view this system is closed and isolated compared to the same environment. To simplify, the law is organised by norms, definable as stabilised normative expectations in logical and coherent form and aimed at congruence. The legal system according to Luhmann operates mechanically by means of an internal function, which allows it to solve some problems regarding social complexity. Decisions coming from such a system are presumed to be legitimate as, once assumed, they are accepted even by those who are subjected to them with cognitive spirit, that is a spirit that abandons expectations, making its own lesson of the facts.

7.1. Sustainable Law Functions

Sustainability law has the characteristic function of solving potential conflicts between norms that aim at promoting commerce and those regarding socio-environmental subjects. From this standpoint, principles of integration, precaution and equity, in line with the principle of sustainable development, integrate concerns for environmental safeguarding with economic and social demands[41] (O'Neill, 1996).

With specific regard to the function of reduction of the complexity and stabilisation of contingency, delineated by Luhmann, it is possible to note that these functions are fully realised in sustainable law. The *corpus* of principles that identifies this law, in effect, carries out clearly within the indicated field this particularly difficult task in which numerous variables of economic, ecological, political and social character meet. Sustainable law, *alias* law in the field of sustainability, confronts itself with the different expectations which converge from several systems, and tries to mediate them and reduce their complexity. Therefore, the systems of social law, environmental law or economic law are "coupled", causing structural modifications, which are made possible by autopoietic actions, through which the same systems re-construct themselves, adding or eliminating elements in view of new functional demands. In the face of these requirements, the legal system will add all the elements that are able to generate more stabilisation in incompatible expectations emerging from the above-mentioned spheres, and will eliminate all those elements that on the contrary tend to be in opposition to such stabilisation, since the latter tend to isolate themselves within their structural complexity and incompatibility. In this way the system of "law to sustainability" that has been created by virtue of these new functional demands and of the operation of "expectations stabilisation", succeeds in reducing the complexity caused by the sum of environmental standards, already highly complex, and the rules coming from the social and economic law sub-systems.

More than in the theoretical aspect, sustainability law in jurisprudence emerges dominantly. It in fact has been able to creatively define different ways of interpreting this particular law.

8. Weak and Strong Visions

The scientific literature on sustainability has generally divided into two scientific strands. The first, called the "strong approach", concerns a vision of environmental sustainability that is mainly ecocentric, which rejects all

[41] From another point of view, in accordance with the ecological and biological perspective related to integrity and sustainability, O'Neill speaks about a "regenerative and reproductive capacity" or "true sustainability".

sorts of integration between the environmental sphere and other spheres, such as the social and economic spheres.

The other strand, however, is the "weak approach", and is mainly linked to an idea of sustainability intended as integration between different spheres and also includes an anthropocentric-utilitarian dimension within it. Therefore, I will proceed by describing in further detail the two differing visions.

9. The "Weak" Vision

Regarding the weak approach to sustainability, it interprets ecological sustainability as a concern separated from social and economic sustainability. With the emergence of economic neo-liberalism, States started to cherry-pick and promoted the weak interpretation of sustainable development, accepted, for example, by authors such as Cordonier Segger, Shrijver, Birnie, Boyle and others.

In this sense, Klaus Bosselmann believes that to consider the ecological, economic and social dimensions of development simultaneously certainly is important, but this in itself does not make development "sustainable"[42] (Bosselmann, 2010, 2437-2438; Bosselmann, 2017, 76-79). This approach interprets sustainable development as interaction between social, economic and ecological interests[43]. In other words, "weak" sustainability shows that sustainable development is where social, economic and ecological interests overlap (Bosselmann, 2006, 43-44). In fact, it accentuates the role of the integration principle and mainly presupposes a more evident anthropocentric perspective, where the "environment" is generally perceived as a static category, which is economically measurable (Bosselmann 2006, 41). This type of sustainability was essentially promoted by the UNCED's work and several governments and corporations.

---

[42] Bosselmann also underlines that any form of development must respect ecological boundaries to avoid decline or collapse.

[43] The experience of New Zealand is relevant: the Resources Management Act (1991) was the world's first legislation based on the principle of sustainability. It requires all economic activities to meet non-negotiable environmental bottom lines. However, in 2014 the Supreme Court of New Zealand rejected this strong approach of sustainability, as not in line with the purpose of the Act.

Also, sources that would seem to justify a strong approach to sustainability, in reality also approach a weak approach. The Brundtland Report, for instance, focuses on the relationship between “human needs” and “limitations”, which are typically anthropocentric concepts. Similarly, the reference to the notion of the “human environment” shown in the Declaration of the United Nations Conference on the Human Environment (Stockholm Declaration, 1972) seems to underline a weak approach to sustainable development. In this sense, some doubts may be advanced with regard to the interpretation of the principle 4 of the Rio Convention. If on the one hand, in effect, an integrative approach could be perceived as a tool aiming at sustainable development in accordance with a weak interpretation, on the other hand, instead, we could intend that development would only be reached by the preservation of nature. In Bosselmann’s opinion, the Brundtland Report does not consider that human needs can only ever be met within ecological boundaries. According to the author, this would open up the possibility of downplaying sustainability (Bosselmann, 2017).

Weak sustainability, contrary to the strong approach, more easily embraces the logic of compromise and integration between different spheres, such as the one between environment and development. Therefore, it indirectly welcomes theories like that of “sustainability science”, which makes the integration between different disciplines the essential methodology of the study of the theoretical branch of sustainability.

Within this weak vision, we could contemplate authors like Cordonier Segger and Khalfan, according to whom sustainable development can be included in the combination of two complementary approaches: in effect, it could be seen both as an emerging area of international law and as a different type of norm, which requires a reconciliation between three areas of law regarding economic development, the protection of the environment and social progress (Cordonier Segger and Khalfan, 2004).

I think that the logic of the compromise characterising the weak approach is not a wrong vision, as it seeks to equitably balance the various inter-human interests, which in any case would also exist in an ecological perspective. However, as I will show later, my vision of sustainability lies in the middle of the two approaches described. Let us also say that environmental law is a kind of mirror in respect to conceptual pillars characterising sustainability. Therefore, I will briefly describe the main anthropocentric characteristics that distinguish environmental sustainability, determined by a utilitarian vision of the natural environment.

An awareness of the consequences that injuries to the environment inflict on the conditions of human life clarifies a possible anthropocentric dimension identifiable within environmental law. A restrictive interpretation of environmental damage and the definition of the common heritage of humankind in my opinion constitute the two main anthropocentric characteristics of environmental law.

9.1. Environmental Damage and the Utilitarian Vision

Considering the economic loss deriving from environmental damage as damage to people and things, and not mainly a damage directed to the environment in the strict sense, would mean considering the environment in an instrumental and utilitarian way. To conceive the environment as a set of natural resources that serve as productive or recreational inputs, whose services are functional to the fulfilment of economic and social welfare utility, would mean to qualify environmental law as a right oriented to the protection of the maximisation of these utilities and not to the protection of the natural environment itself. An example is the utility supplied from water or the wood from trees. From this particular point of view, we could say that environmental law, thus conceived, has a strictly utilitarian purpose. In line with this utilitarian view, it is logical to assume that a compensation for damage to the environment is equivalent to a compensation due to a person for the loss of the economic or social utilities that occurred due to the damage, e.g., the economic injury suffered. Therefore, the value of the environment would seem to be related to the nature of compromises of human rights.

The legislation on the "environmental damage" that considers it a reflection of damage to property or people, in consequence of which economic damage is caused, contributes to the analytical study of the first nature that identifies the "two-faced personality" of environmental law, seen under an anthropocentric and utilitarian key, as instrumental to the well-being of a human being. Let us first state that the value of an environment, not infrequently, is captured at the moment when that environment is damaged. The problem relating to the assessment of a given environment is a matter that should at first be resolved with reference to the definition of environmental damage. Depending on the interpretation we give to this definition, in fact, we can have another definition of assessment which, sometimes, according to a strict interpretation, refers to a compensation for the purely economic loss suffered by the injured and, sometimes, with a wider interpretation, concerns the assessment of the decrease in value of the damaged environmental resource, where the concept of *restitutio in integrum* gains a primary importance because its aim is precisely to give back to the environment the lost value caused by the occurrence of the damage.

The restrictive interpretation of the environmental damage, interesting us herewith, has characterised the environment for some time and presupposes the definition of resource or environmental good as *res nullius*, so that when the damage occurs, what is considered as harmed and therefore compensable is not the considered resource itself but rather the possible economic damage that may have been caused to one or more parties as a result of that damage. Such a prejudice has been framed in the jurisprudence not only as a financial loss in the strict sense, but as a broader concept[44]. According to this orientation, the greater the decrease of values or economic utilities from which the harmed person could benefit, the more consistent the extent of the environmental damage that would be quantified. In this context, the Amoco-Cadiz lawsuit is very significant. The judges here did nothing but implicitly propose a restrictive notion of environmental damage, which qualified the environmental resource as *res nullius*. On the night of March 21, 1978, the Amoco-Cadiz[45] oil tanker sank in the Breton Department of North-Finestère: more than 220,000 tons of crude oil spilled in marine waters causing a real environmental disaster. The Court excluded the recoverability of the damage that had been caused by the annihilation of the fish species in the oil spill area, justifying this position by the fact that the expert report related to the damage to the biomass had not led to convincing and incontrovertible results. The focal point of the judgment is that in which the Court denied the recoverability of the ecological damage, due to the nature of the damaged resource as *res nullius,* with the result that no person could consider himself entitled to claim compensation. At this point it seems appropriate to quote the expressions used by the Court to express this concept: "The Court has heard the extensive testimony concerning the biomass, the totality of life in the sea and on the bottom in the affected zone. The biomass valuation was complex, attenuated, speculative, and reached conclusions based upon a chain of assumptions, a deficiency in any one of which would dramatically affect the final result. The Court need not grapple however with this damage question because of its conclusion that this

---

[44] See for example the judgment of the Italian Court of Cassation, according to which the concept of economic injury concerns eligibility to determine specifically a decrease in economic values and utilities of which an injured person may have (Civil Cass, Section I, 9 April 1992, n. 4362).

[45] Lexis-1988 U.S. Dist. Lexis 16832.

claimed damage is subject to the principle of *res nullius* and is not compensable for lack of standing of any person or entity to claim therefore".

If the claims for compensation to common Bretons were not taken into account by the Court as founded "upon the damage to a legal interest in protecting the maritime public domain", those advanced by fishermen who saw the quantities fished and therefore sold reduced, however, were considered as legitimate. Even the resettlement plans for certain species presented by some scientists were deliberately neglected by the Court as to the judges this was a project aimed at improving the ecosystem of the area and not directed to recreate the situation that was existing before the accident. In this case, it is clear that they did not consider the decreased value of the damaged resource, but the economical prejudice resulting from the damage.

From another point of view, the underestimation of the good "environment", represented by the promotion of the pollution generated by certain production activities, is well exemplified in the following lawsuits. In the lawsuit *Turner vs. Big Lake Oil Co* (1936)[46] the Court refused to apply the *tort of strict liability* and hence the principle of strict liability. In this case the defendant built a basin, afferent to its oil wells, from which a fluid able to cause damage flowed; despite this, the judge acknowledged that "oil is big business in Texas", and it is on that business that social welfare depends.

We can put on the same level the lawsuit *Boomer vs. Atlantic Cement Co.* (1967)[47], where the Boomers went before the Supreme Court of Albany and demanded the cessation of the *nuisances* together with the compensation for the damage, as the Atlantic Cement Co. was supposed to be responsible for various types of pollution. The Court, while acknowledging that the applicants were entitled to request the status of *the tort of nuisance*, decided that the injunction in this case could not be granted because heavy investment had been borne by the defendant and, moreover, a large number of people had found employment thanks to the same activity. Therefore, the judge merely granted the *damage* only. On appeal, Judge Bergan, after having widely criticised the management of the environmental policies, which in his opinion should not have been devolved to the judiciary power but to the federal government only, argued that: "the total damage to plaintiffs' properties is, however, relatively small in comparison with the value of defendant's operation and with the consequences of the injunction

---

[46] Court of Texas, *Turner vs. Big Lake Oil Co.* 96, 1936.
[47] Court of New York, *Boomer vs. Atlantic Cement Co.*, 287, 1967.

which plaintiffs seek". An example of this would be the lawsuit *Fritz vs. E. Du Pont de Nemours & Co.* (1950)[48] where a railway employee claimed damage caused by a gas (chlorine gas) leak, asking for compensation: The Court of Delaware affirmed that "it was not unlawful for Du Pont to have on its premises chlorine gas, nor was its presence there unusual, and it cannot be said that the mere possession of chlorine gas by Du Pont (…) was dangerous per se in the light of recognized industrial use".

See also the request for compensation subsequent to the alleged economic loss suffered during the environmental damage that the regional committee of the Breton tourism and Loire Valley presented to *the Tribunal de Grande Instance of Rennes* in 2000 against the oil company Total-Final Elf[49]. Following The Erika's sinking, in fact, that company, just to cancel out the perplexities that might arise with reference to the opportunity to visit those areas or not, simply transmitted the images depicting the effects of the shipwreck through the mass media. For the Regional Tourism Committee this gesture would have the sole effect of further damaging the image of the areas affected by the damage, leading to a series of adverse economic effects, especially with reference to tourism.

9.2. The Common Heritage of Humanity and the Anthropocentric Vision

Even the concept of the "common heritage of humanity" would contain an anthropocentric dimension and therefore fall in accordance with a weak vision of sustainability.

The notion of "heritage" evidently refers to an anthropocentric perspective, although it is a "common" heritage and theoretically "sharable". In this case, the owner of the rights is not a single person or a group of individuals, nor is it even nature; rather it is the entire human race.

The Committee of experts for the progressive codification of international law entrusted the writing of a report on international norms concerning the exploitation of living marine resources to the Argentinian jurist José Léon Suárez. He proposed that such resources, with particular consideration for whales, had to be considered a heritage of humankind. In the report presented in 1927, Suárez stressed the necessity of giving life to a new type

---

[48] Court of Delaware, Fritz *vs*. E. Du Pont de Nemours & Co, 1950.

[49] Tribunal de Grande Instance de Rennes, 18 December 2000, in *Recueil Le Dalloz*, n. 9, 2001.

of treaty, which would be able to prevent the destruction of living resources. For this purpose, he suggested summoning an international conference to establish and implement the principle by which whales and other living marine resources could belong to this heritage.

The idea of a "common heritage of humanity", instead, was expressed in a speech held on the occasion of the General Assembly of the United Nations on November 1st 1967 by the representative of Malta, Arvid Pardo. The opportunity to suggest a completely new system was allowed by technological developments that would have led, in a relatively short time, to the commercial exploitation of polymetallic nodules lying on the surface of the seabed, which contained minerals such as manganese, nickel, cobalt and copper. Often, however, the concept of humankind common heritage implies a "common human worry" or "common concern", which obliges States to cooperate so as to prevent an imminent risk on assets subject to common property. Other times, instead, it refers to the sharing of benefits in the exploitation of certain resources.

10. The "Strong" Vision

With regard to a strong approach, I would like to anticipate that in the definition of "sustainable development" proposed by the famous Brundtland Report (1987) – the Report of the World Commission on Environment and Development (Our Common Future) – ecological sustainability is assumed as the most important element of the concept, since it shows the Earth's ecological integrity as the prerequisite for development. This sets limits to both economic and social development. In this sense, therefore, ecology would play a prominent role, society would be part of ecology, and the economy a part of both systems (Bosselmann, 2002, 81-91)[50]. In addition to this report, further sources are relevant in this context, such as the Earth Charter, which underlines preservation of the integrity of ecological systems, and the Millennium Declaration, which focuses on respect of nature.

This approach is based on a non-anthropocentric view, namely an ecocentric vision, according to which trade-offs between economy and environment should be prohibited. In other words, according to supporters of a strong approach, if the sustainability of ecological systems is primary, therefore "it sets a non-negotiable absolute negative to any form of development" (Bosselmann, 2016, 27). Therefore, generally, the logic of

---

[50] This is shown by the image of the "nested egg".

the compromise or the possibility of integration between economic development and the environmental sphere is not willingly accepted by the representatives of an ecocentric vision corresponding to a strong sustainability[51] (Preston, 2016, 479).

Moreover, from an ecological point of view, anthropocentric conceptions of the future would be difficult to justify and thus the future generation rights branch would be not very appreciable in accordance with a strong approach, because the concern would in any case fall on human beings (Bosselmann, 2010, 2438). In my opinion, instead, the future generations branch is fundamental, since it intends to propose an anthropological link between human beings and their own life environment. Ulrich Beyerlin, in this regard, concludes that "as intergenerational equity is inseparably intertwined with intra-generational equity, the concept of sustainable development in its entirety must be perceived as both anthropocentric and eco-centric in nature" (Beyerlin, 2006, 259-296).

Douglas Fisher, in his book *Legal Reasoning in Environmental Law*, studied the approach of politicians/administrators and judges in respect to environmental issues, showing how they generally focus on economic tools, such as welfare, cost-benefit analysis and so on. In this view, environmental interests are very often bound to lose against hard economic interests, because the anthropocentric perspective dominates (Fisher, 2013, 433). From another point of view, Andrew Dobson wrote that the ecocentric approach marks the point at which economists usually leave the sustainability debate (Dobson, 1996, 401-416). Finnis, for his part, links sustainability to the ability to "sustain" the natural conditions upon which life depends. Bosselmann too argues that in pursuing the protection of ecological integrity, sustainability reflects the most basic concern of human existence, that is to say the desire to live, survive[52] and reproduce (Bosselmann, 2016, 44). He underlines further that ecological

---

[51] Even if some exceptions exist. For instance, Brian J. Preston, a supporter of the strong vision believes that the concept of ecologically sustainable development can be related to three different legislative and policy instruments. In effect, the second group of tools presupposes an effective integration of economic and environmental considerations in decision-making processes.

[52] This is true, even if the very concept of "survival" is clearly an anthropocentric concept. Nevertheless, it is the ultimate goal of ethically sustainable development, because it is the right to sustain the natural conditions against which life is dependent.

sustainability is the fundament for development and not a mere 'pillar' (Bosselmann, 2016, 29).

As Bosselmann recalls, the duty to protect the integrity of Earth's ecological systems is expressed in no less than 25 international agreements, from the 1982 World Charter for Nature rights through to the 2015 Paris Climate Agreement. Principle 7 of the 1992 Rio Declaration requires States to cooperate in the spirit of global partnership. Art. 20 a) of the German Constitution too requires the State to protect the natural foundations of all life[53] (Bosselmann, 2010, 2437).

The concept of the "Anthropocene" seems to be moving the balance towards the strong approach to sustainability. This concept was introduced by Nobel Laureate Paul Crutzen. It concerns the possibility that the Earth has entered a new geological epoch. This age is characterised by hard pervasive human impacts on the world, as well as increased levels of instability and unpredictability. This concept certainly pushes towards a reconstruction of relationships between human beings and the environment, which must be considered as a living environment and not an abstract entity.

From the this viewpoint, resilience can be seen as "a core principle to guide social behavior in adapting to the conditions of the Anthropocene" (Robinson, 2014, 20). The main change that the Anthropocene entails would be the effect on human choices:

> "We will make political choices about who will gain and who will lose (or perhaps more accurately, who will lose most and who will lose less) from the transition to the Anthropocene. We will make political choices about how proactive to be in responding to the Anthropocene, or whether we will play catch-up, putting even greater pressures on our legal, social, political and economic systems. Whatever political choice we make, the legal landscape will never be the same" (Biber, 2017, 68).

Moreover, as Kotzé reports, different versions of the Anthropocene Era exist. One version concerns the "Great Acceleration", which details the decline of Earth System integrity that is linked to a rise in greenhouse gas emissions, increased industrialisation and biodiversity loss, consumption, population growth, and urbanisation, in addition to a mass extinction. Another version, instead, sees human domination of the Earth System as our

---

[53] The German medieval land use system (*Allmende*) has been considered as the mother of sustainable economies. In effect, the first law based on the sustainability principle was the Weimar Forestry Statute (1775) in Germany.

disruption of the planetary boundaries that determine the self-regulating capacity of the Earth System (Kotzé, 2019, 3).

Earth system law can be summarised as a new research agenda "that is able to respond to the unique epistemic, ontological and normative characteristics, demands and nature of earth system governance in the Anthropocene" (Kotzé and Kim, 2019, 2).

This law would be both a descriptive and prescriptive concept. In a descriptive sense, it "could more meaningfully embrace the juridical aspects of earth system governance, while, conversely, earth system law could introduce earth system governance as a research and regulatory concern into the science of law". In a prescriptive sense, instead, it "should be more closely aligned with the Anthropocene's normative demands to the extent that it seeks to improve the ability of law to better respond to the deeply intertwined Earth system and its many complex socio-ecological challenges" (Kotzé and Kim, 2019, 2).

In line with this vision, the Anthropocene metaphor is seen as a new metanarrative, or rather, as a broad context within which to contemplate the law's role. "Anthropocene law" would fall into three sub-categories: environmental law, which focuses on the human dimension; ecological law, that is focused on nature; and, last but not least, earth law, which is centred on the earth.

According to Kotzé and Kim (2019), the Earth System Governance Project's new Science and Implementation Plan provides an opportunity to rethink a different legal paradigm for law. Despite this, the concept of the Anthropocene has been criticised anyway in its legal dimension (see e.g., Westra, 2016, 91-93).

10.1. Earth Jurisprudence (or Wild Law) and Ecological Law

In the wake of the approach described above, some schools of thought and study have arisen, such as that of Earth Jurisprudence (also called Wild Law) and that of Ecological Law.

Both visions find their own roots in deep ecology philosophy and a strong vision refusing every form of anthropocentrism.

The strong vision of environmental sustainability is greatly welcomed by the Ecological Law and Governance Association, founded by Klaus Bosselmann, whose perspective I have already summarised. This association promotes the strong approach through ecological law, which confers centrality to the ecological dimension, diversifying itself from environmental law.

The "*Oslo Manifesto*" for Ecological Law and Governance Association (June 2016) is a representative document describing ecological law. Par. VI of this Manifesto in fact underlines that "ecological law reverses the principle of human dominance over nature, which the current interaction of environmental law tends to reinforce".

For its part, Wild Law or Earth Jurisprudence is an emerging theory of law requiring a deep rethinking of the human position within the world.

Alexander Gillespie identified some anthropocentric justifications related to environmental protection, such as self-interest, religion, economics, culture, aesthetics and future generations (Gillespie, 1997).

Bosselmann underlines the passage from environmental law to ecological law, as a passage that reflects an "ethical dilemma", orienting environmental law in an ecocentric sense (Kim and Bosselmann, 2013, 285). This is a position that welcomes the intrinsic value of nature and, in contrast to many other standpoints, condemns any use and exploitation of nature, conceiving the natural ecosystems to which man also belongs in a holistic way.

Anthropocentrism, in its own character undifferentiated to humankind, lurks behind some realities of human and social life (Malm and Hornborg, 2014, 62). The very attribute "environmental" would indicate the dominance of a human dimension.

From another point of view, the link between human rights and natural rights is undeniable and therefore so is the anthropocentric character that derives from it.

For Anna Grear, the "Anthropos" is the universal representation of mankind: it is "far removed from human being in any rich and inclusive sense" (Grear, 2013, 82). In this regard, she speaks about "vectors of oppression linking intra and inter-species hierarchies" (Grear, 2013, 234).

Taking a positive view of a limited threshold of anthropocentrism has given way to various concepts, such as that of "weak anthropocentrism" that was promoted by Bryan Norton to make anthropocentrism a valid alternative to ecocentrism (Norton 1984, 131), or the "stewardship" concept concerning the responsible use of natural resources in a way that considers several needs of society (Worrell and Applleby, 1999, 263).

After all, ecocentrism, as well as anthropocentrism, is subject to "centrism", that is, to the epistemology of the centre. On this, Philippopoulos-Mihalopoulos speaks of the "tyranny of the center" (Philippopoulos-Mihalopoulos, 2011, 29; Philippopoulos-Mihalopoulos 2013, 857).

Among the supporters of ecocentrism, instead, we find a deep ecologist, Thomas Berry, who in 1999 in his work *The Great Work: Our Way into the Future* suggested a "new jurisprudence", that is to say a new way of governing ourselves in the face of twenty-first century challenges, in order to protect the integrity of the Earth system. According to Berry, the causes of the ecological crisis are to be recognised exactly in anthropocentrism; hence, the need for a new jurisprudence (Earth Jurisprudence) would follow. He develops some ideas by Aldo Leopold, Arne Naess and George Sessions, as well as Christopher Stone. Berry argued that every member of the Earth Community had some rights, as the right to be or the right to habitat.

In line with the "Earth Jurisprudence", the Universe is the main lawgiver and its rights provide the pillars of the Earth Community. These rights generate relations between humanity and the Earth Community, aimed at the continuation of an "evolutionary journey" of the members of this Community (Berry, 1999).

The rights arising from Earth Jurisprudence include the rights to exist, to habitat, and to contribute to the evolution of the Earth Jurisprudence (Berry, 2002).

Nature rights for Berry should be pre-existent, compared to human rights, as they have been created by the very act of the Universe. In order to link an ecocentric vision with the social sphere, "Earth Democracy" has been invoked within this framework (Burdon 2014).

Given that every form of life (human and nonhuman) is connected to the Earth, every living being would have a right to exist and to develop.

As Michelle Maloney and Sister Patricia Siemen claim, "under an Earth Jurisprudence approach, human rights are an interdependent and correlative subset of Earth rights, humanity cannot be healthy and secure if Earth is veering towards depletion and over-extraction" (Maloney and Siemen, 2015, 12).

Cormac Cullinan urged embracing our compassion, love and spirit to Earth, as it exists within us (Cullinan, 2002). From this point of view, the theoretical premise of Earth Jurisprudence would basically reside in the separation between the Universe and human activities, in the sense that for centuries we humans have been committed to build a world separate from the very existence of the Universe. According to Burdon, Earth Jurisprudence develops by a critique of "any law, legal system, jurisprudence that allows the surpassing of ecological limits of the environment to satisfy needs of any one species" (Burdon, 2011, 15).

Within this strong vision, therefore, the theory of the "rights of nature" is essential to describe the "environment" as a direct beneficiary of legal rules.

10.2. The Rights of Nature

The study of the rights of nature shows how environmental law has known theoretical processes that have made the environment the only true recipient of legal rules. In literature, it is customary to distinguish between "*legal rights*" and "*moral rights*": this distinction has developed mainly in the Anglo-Saxon tradition. Norberto Bobbio, in contrast, believes that such a distinction is incomprehensible, since law and morality are two very different spheres of practical life. The expression "legal rights" would sound redundant, and the concept of "moral rights" would be rather contradictory. The differences between the two types of rights may be understood with reference to the subjective conditions of ownership (Bobbio, 1990).

With regard to the above-mentioned "legal rights", we can well quote Stone. He in effect proposes that a "guardian of nature" can exercise the rights granted to nature itself. Stone, adopting the distinction between natural objects and legal persons, finds that if rights can be granted to *trusts* and companies, such a granting could be addressed to natural goods. If it is true that such goods do not utter a word, just like companies, it is equally true that they can benefit from "fiduciary representatives" who are acting in their best interest. With reference to the above, Stone suggests that a "friend" of natural goods, such as an environmental organisation, could strive to promote the role of "guardian of the environment". In *Should Trees Have Standing? Toward Legal Rights for Natural Objects,* Stone wanted to prove that the concept of law can also be easily adapted to natural objects (Stone, 1974).

The law generally distinguishes between legal capacity and capacity to act. One can indeed have rights without being able to exercise the appropriate action to protect them. In this case, the function to assert the rights of the subject without capacity to act is delegated to a representative. In this perspective, the jurisprudential tendency beginning in the '70s in the United States is worth highlighting. The Sierra Club, one of the major US environmental organisations, appealed against an order issued by the US Forest Service who had granted permission to the *Walt Disney Enterprises* to use for tourist-commercial purposes the *Mineral King Valley*, a protected area located in the mountain range of the *Sierra Nevada* in California. The US Supreme Court had established that the Sierra Club had no right to start the litigation, in so much that it was only entitled to defend the interests of its members and not those of nature. However, Judge Douglas considered that the question concerning the legal status of nature would be better addressed through the development of standards that authorised the examination of environmental cases by agencies or federal Courts in the name of the natural objects. The Court upheld the idea of the rights of nature, given that the cause was functional to the exclusive interest of nature itself. In the perspective of the rights of nature, moreover, the judge should always consider the damage objectively caused to the ecosystem, disregarding any economic prejudice: the compensation, again, should be used to the advantage of the damaged environment and not in favour of any owner of such an environment. The subjective interest of the holder of the environmental law does not necessarily meet with the objective interest of the environment itself. In a way, Judge Douglas promoted a new federal rule and thus a new jurisprudential tendency, which recognises a modern figure of a guardian or legal representative acting on behalf of and in the interests of the natural goods (Douglas 1972, 27).

In 2008, Ecuador became the first country to include rights of nature in its Constitution, including the right to integral respect for its existence and for the maintenance and regeneration of its life cycles, functions, structure and evolutionary processes, as well as the right to be restored.

The "rights of nature" were recognised in the Universal Declaration on the Rights of Mother Earth in Cochabamba, Bolivia, in 2010.

A 2011 ruling by a provincial court in Ecuador recognises the Vilcabamba River's rights, which can be considered a civil party in order to defend itself against the threat of overbuilding[54].

In India, on 1 April 2017, the Himalayan Gangotri and Yamunotri glaciers were granted the status of living entities, given their meadows, lakes, waterfalls and forests. Similarly, on 20 March 2017, the Ganga and Yamuna rivers were granted human status. In effect, in the judgement "Mohd. Salim *vs.* State of Uttarakhand & Others", after noting a deep spiritual connection between Hindus and the Rivers Ganga and Yamuna, the Court mentioned several previous cases where the notion of legal personality has been considered. In the case "Lalit Miglani *vs.* State of Uttarakhand & Others", the Uttarakhand Hight Court extended the borders of legal personality even further to encompass the "Glaciers including Gangotri and Yamunotri, rivers, streams, rivulets, lakes, air, meadows, dales, jungles, forests, wetlands, grasslands, springs and waterfalls", declaring several individuals to be persons in loco parentis of these entities in Uttarakhand State.

On 28 January 2017, the Constitution of Mexico City adopted the rights of nature in article 13, paragraphs 2 and 3.

In New Zealand, a national park that on 27 July 2014 became "Te Urewera", namely a legal entity with all the rights, duties, powers and liabilities of a legal person. It is managed by a board that is responsible for acting on behalf of, and in the name of, Te Urewera. Moreover, in March 2017, the New Zealand government passed legislation to give the Whanganui river legal personality (Bosselmann 2006, 163-166). This finds its logical base in the notion of "kaitiakitanga", a Maori concept that means "guardianship"[55].

In this framework, even several political sources are relevant, such as two IUCN Resolutions (078 and 089) adopted at the IUCN World Conservation Congress on 1-10 September 2016, as well as the IUCN Programme 2017-2020.

Regan also agrees with the point of view of the rights of nature (Regan, 1983; Nash, 1989). Similarly, Passmore considers that if animals are holders of rights, natural goods should also be holders in the same way, as these

[54] From this point of view, Chapter VII of Ecuador Constitution is fundamental.

[55] I also recall an Indian decision about the status of legal persons for the Ganga and Yamuna rivers. In this sense, another Indian Court similarly decided for the Himalayan Mountains, rivers, lakes, glaciers, forests and so on, underlining that the rights of these entities shall be equivalent to the rights of human beings.

goods can be protected by the law, not as mere objects of property (Passmore, 1980).

The concept of the "moral rights of nature" differs from the purely legal connotations, hiding in fact a moral sense. In the case of so called "legal rights" of nature, in fact, the legitimacy is based on the law or the rules and regulations, while for the "moral rights" this legitimacy would recognise its *ratio* in a principle of moral nature. When talking about moral rights of nature, Regan, for example, argues about natural rights (in the classic sense of "natural law"). Similarly, according to Robin Attfield living creatures having interests (including animals and plants) have rights and therefore must not suffer violence (Attfield, 1981).

We also have to consider that with reference to the ethics of the rights of nature, several objections have been addressed that it is useful to mention here below. A first objection can be found in the equivocalness of the language of the rights which is not suitable for a non-human environment (Taylor, 1986). A second objection has been put forward by Norton, according to whom the logic of rights would have the risk of increasing the claims to be satisfied, enough to make the resolution of the litigations more complex (Norton 1982, 17-36).

A third objection, however, is represented by people like Passmore and Watson, believing that the ownership of rights is functional to the ownership of certain duties (Passmore, 1980; Watson 1979). According to the principle of reciprocity of commitments, these relationships would buy significance to the extent that they are marked by mutual commitments. This principle is in line with the contractual model of morality, according to which morality is seen as a set of rules individuals voluntarily accept to adapt to, in the same manner in which you engage yourself when signing a contract. Rawls, for example, denies that the contractors have direct duties to those who do not have the ability to discern right from wrong: compared to them, in fact, we would not be obliged to do justice in a strict manner (Rawls, 1999).

A further objection to the rights of nature is also proposed by Taylor and McCloskey, who argue that to discuss the rights of non-humans would mean to open the way to a conceptual confusion (Taylor, 1986). Taylor and Norton, again, indicate that having interests does not necessarily imply having rights. Norton, for his part, highlights the individualistic nature of the concept of moral rights: the rights would be the prerogative of individually identifiable entities (Norton, 1982). Gunn also underlines the highly individualistic nature of the examined concept. In addition, some even considered it unnecessary to talk about the rights of the environment: Rescher, for example, notes that the assignment of rights to nature presupposes a correlation between rights and duties that does not always exist (Rescher, 1983). In this sense we could say that we have a duty not to pollute a waterway, but not that this resource has the right not to be polluted.

For the Strasbourg Court the environment is a "value". We recall in this regard the following lawsuits: *Taşkın et al. vs. Turkey*[56] (2004), *Moreno Gómez vs. Spain*[57] (2004), Fadeïeva *vs. Russia*[58] (2005) and *Giacomelli vs. Italia*[59] (2006). The environmental protection for the Court is "a value, the defence of which arouses a constant and steady interest of public opinion, and as a consequence public authorities. Economic imperatives and even some fundamental rights, like the right of property, should not been granted primacy ahead of considerations relating to environmental protection, in particular when the State has legislated on the subject"[60].

With reference to this, we can also cite the judgment of 30 December 1987, n. 641[61] of the Italian Constitutional Court, which states that "in our legal system the protection of the environment (...) becomes the primary and absolute value". The jurisprudence of the Constitutional Court is now unanimous in describing the environment as of constitutional value[62].

Later, the Italian Court confirmed that the environment in the legal sense should be considered as a whole. Although including several goods or values, such as flora, fauna, soil and water, it is ontologically distinguished from these, as it would identify itself in a reality devoid of material substance, but at the same time expressive of an autonomous collective value that is independent from the concept of prejudice (judgment no. 4362 of 1992).

---

[56] *Taskin et al. vs. Turkey*, App. No. 46117/99, 2004-X Eur. Ct. H.R.
[57] *Moreno Gómez vs. Spain*, App. No. 4143/02, 2004-X Eur. Ct. H.R.
[58] *Fadeïeva vs. Russia*, App. No. 55723/00, 2005-IV Eur. Ct. H.R.
[59] *Giacomelli vs. Italy*, App. No. 59909/00, 2006-XII Eur. Ct. H.R.
[60] *Köktepe vs. Turkey*, App. No. 35785/03, 2007 Eur. Ct. H.R.
[61] Italian Constitutional Court, 30 December 1987, n. 641, in Foro Italiano, 1988, I: 694.
[62] Constitutional Court, 18 March 2005, n. 108; Constitutional Court 22 July 2004, n. 259; Constitutional Court 28 June 2004, n. 196; Constitutional Court 4 July 2003, n. 227; Constitutional Court 24 June 2003, n. 222; Constitutional Court 20 December 2002, n. 536; Constitutional Court 26 July 2002, n. 407.

Within this "value dimension", furthermore, and relating to the matter of "environmental damage", we should consider that if the law focuses on measures that attempt to give back to the environment its lost value, then the same environment is the direct recipient of the juridical efficacy of environmental law provisions.

In the Convention of the Council of Europe on civil liability for environmental damage from hazardous activities, ratified in Lugano in June 1993, damage was defined as a deterioration of the environment to the extent that this did not consist in damage to property or people, but provided that such degradation however caused a loss of economic gain. With reference to this setting, direct damage to the environment coincided with the cost of preventive measures and of refurbishing, adopted in order to contain, minimise or restore the situation prior to the offense. If *restitutio in integrum* had been impossible from a technical standpoint, the introduction into the environment of resources equivalent to those which had been destroyed could be imposed on the tortfeasor. In the case where instead this *restitutio* had not been possible due to the final disappearance, determined by the damage of an animal or plant species, the Convention excluded that it could generate a type of financial compensation. In the *Explanatory Report* (European Council, doc. Nr. 1 01/26/1993) accompanying the text of the Convention we can see that direct damage to the environment per se was not susceptible to economic evaluation: "such damage cannot be evaluated financially"; however, in the face of the impossibility of restoring the environment damaged or destroyed, the Convention decided for the option to re-create a similar environment.

With the "White Paper on environmental liability", presented by the European Commission in February 2000 [COM (2000) 66 final], the discipline of environmental responsibility emerged for its compensatory purpose and not for the punitive one. Therefore, the environmental damage assessment criteria will have to be structured in a way to represent only the value of the natural resources and the lost services.

With the EC Directive 2004/35/EC the *restitutio in integrum* acquires an established status, which has to be interpreted as the prevalent criterion on other measures, so that we talk about "primary", "complementary" and "compensatory" remedial measures. As primary remediation, we quote any remedial measure that brings the resources and/or impaired natural services to, or towards, the original conditions. If those resources and services do not return to these conditions, complementary remediation will be undertaken, which aims to obtain, if necessary, at an alternative site, a level of natural resources and/or services similar to those you would have had if the damaged site had been returned to its original conditions. A compensatory restoration, instead, is given to compensate for the temporary loss of natural resources and services while waiting for the recovery. The compensation consists of additional improvements to the protected species and to the natural habitats, to the water in the damaged site or in an alternative one. Annex II to the Directive also considers that if it is not possible to use as first choice the equivalency methods of "resource-to-resource" or "service-to-service", then alternative valuation techniques should be used. The referenced Directive, in fact, describes a hierarchy of remedial measures, and does not consider the equitable assessment of the damage. This source undoubtedly suffers the influence both of the Lugano Convention, of the Explanatory Report and of the "White Paper". Thanks to this Directive, various valuation methodologies of environmental damage already experienced in the United States have been developed in Europe. These methodologies are based on equivalence criteria of the resources[63] that allow the selection of the recovery measures on the basis of obtaining benefits equivalent to those previously granted by the damaged resource[64].

11. Balanced Sustainability and Justice

Supporting ecological, human and social living conditions is the main task of sustainability, which therefore projects the logical structure of justice into space and time. This justice should be examined by an ethical sense that goes beyond the mere category of Rawlsian justice and the theoretical canons of global and planetary justice. Obviously, it is also an interspecies justice between human and non-human species.

In this dimension, the "environment" is certainly an important element belonging to this theoretical framework, since it is not a static category, principally referring to natural resources that can be economically measured. Nevertheless, the value of the environment cannot be represented only by the values of non-use (intrinsic value or existence value). The dependence of man on certain natural resources in fact is undeniable and

---

[63] In the European context, about the methods of equivalence we can mention the project "REMEDE" (*Resource Equivalence Methods for Assessing Environmental Damage in the EU*).

[64] In other words, these methods are designed to translate in economic terms the value of the benefits and services of environmental resources, by estimating the costs of travel and/or subrogation, the hedonic pricing, contingent valuation, conjoint choice, and the benefit transfer.

inevitably welcomes the utilitarian dimension represented by the science of values represented by the values of use. In this regard, just think of water as a resource, without which man and every other life form would cease to exist; hence, the value of use (or option value) of this resource is of decisive importance. Therefore, the very fact that humanity depends on ecological integrity leads us to necessarily consider an anthropocentric matrix in sustainable development. This however does not mean not considering the intrinsic value and the same ability of the environment, but only reconciling human needs with a healthy environment, in accordance with a fair balance between Earth and humankind. The environment is the ability to link one to the other, because there is no development without ecological integrity.

Furthermore, future generations risk receiving from the current and previous generations an increasingly damaged land, characterised by highly polluted natural resources that are prone to exhaustion. Therefore, the theoretical branch relating to future generations should not be read through the magnifying glass of anthropocentrism and therefore excluded from ecological rationality.

A "justice for sustainability" needs a responsibility that is mainly embodied in value-based, common, equitable and intergenerational responsibilities, where ample space is given to virtues and integrity (moral and ecological). The governance of a sustainable justice is a multilateral, multilevel, polycentric and cooperative governance, as well as being inclusive, integrative and equitable. Within this scenario, sustainability law is based on a meta-legal, holistic and moral nature[65], and it is recognisable as a customary norm with a strictly interdisciplinary character (Grasso, 2015).

Remaining always in the perspective of justice, I have been recently proposing the foundation of a "critical justice", capable of facing a crisis connected to the climate emergency in a new way. This justice wants to spread awareness on the dramatic effects of moral and political nihilism, adopting a critical and equitable philosophy of emergency. Indeed it seeks to recover human and social dignity, since this dignity is often compromised

---

[65] The principle of sustainability could be understood as a moral basic norm or rather as a "*grundnorm*". Ecological protection, in fact, should be promoted as a "*grundnorm*" (a basic norm), with respect to which sustainability law is very important. Therefore, the basic norm is no longer seen according to the Kelsenian vision as an epistemological premise, but in accordance with a Kantian vision, which considers the basic norm to be a reasonable premise able to prevent the legal arbitrary will (see Bosselmann, 2017).

because of several individual and collective human actions, such as the emissions of greenhouse gases, and especially due to global systems of power (Grasso, 2019).

12. My Vision of Sustainability

My vision of 'sustainability' goes beyond the mere bipartition between a 'weak' and a 'strong' approach to sustainable development and it is placed within a 'balanced sustainability', which lies between a moderate ecocentric vision and a weak anthropocentric perspective (Grasso, 2015). This approach could be defined as a "semi-strong" approach to sustainability. In other words, my sustainability vision finds its best form of expression in the ethics of the relationship between nature and human beings in order to mediate the opposing positions of strong anthropocentrism and radical biocentrism. Indeed, this view rejects both an absolute anthropocentrism and an extremist perspective of ecocentrism, which places in the foreground the moral primacy of nature as a supreme living organism.

A culture of sustainable development presupposes a new way of thinking and living in the world and requires the responsible and aware modification of behaviours and lifestyles and therefore a "new anthropocentrism", which we could qualify as responsible or aware anthropocentrism. It includes in itself the reasons of ethics, anthropology, ecology, law and human and social development, directing them towards claims of social equity and justice, so that economic development is compatible with the protection of the life environment and society as a whole (Grasso, 2015).

Therefore, I do not see the possibility of the "compromise" in a negative way, if this obviously does not take the form of merely a purely utilitarian attempt to give the impression of undertaking some "sustainable" manifestation, for the exclusive purpose of obtaining a return of image[66]. The compromise is morally permissible if it becomes an ethical means of creating a bridge between human and social development and ecology. Indeed, the integration of various dimensions could even be a moral advantage able to increase the sense of humanity in harmony with the surrounding environment.

---

[66] Often, companies use corporate social responsibility tools only for the purpose of creating a positive image in public opinion that could increase their profits.

This vision is confronted with environmental and health emergencies. It is mainly linked to catastrophic emergencies, such as those connected to extreme events, so much so that I recently theorised a new branch of sustainability. In effect, my vision recently has been moving towards a new theoretical interpretation that goes in the direction of an 'emergency' dimension, dealing with the study of humanitarian, ethical, environmental, health and social emergencies, which are particularly connected to extreme events, catastrophes and more generally to every "crisis situation". In this sense, I have argued for a new branch of sustainability (*Emergency Sustainability*), that aims to overcome the classic bipartition between 'weak' and 'strong' sustainability, while also contemplating a series of concepts, such as those of "epistemic health" (Grasso, 2019) and "responsible catastrophism" (Grasso, 2017), which give a certain ethical direction to this particular sustainable vision. Furthermore, the protection of natural resources is increasingly compromised, as is the protection of vulnerable populations who are faced with the consequences of emergencies deriving from climate change and the numerous disasters that often occur unexpectedly.

SECTION 2

RESILIENCE AND THE LAW

1. Introduction

Sustainability law has been developing to the point of making room for the notion of "resilience", which in effect is progressively emerging. This evolution will be described through some particular theoretical branches, such as the theories on legal change. This section will try to address several theoretical issues related to the concept of resilience and the role of law in this context.

A homogeneous framework on resilience should be filtered by an equitable theoretical matrix. The relationship between resilience, sustainability, law and equity, as well as the link between resilience, global complexity and justice will be clarified in the last part of this work.

2. Resilience and Theoretical Perspectives: Sustainable Development as a Necessary Conceptual – Logical Premise

At the European level, sustainable development is a principle of constitutional nature, both programmatic and judicial, qualified precisely as a principle and objective[67] of European Community action and placed

[67] The qualification of the sustainable development principle as an objective to be pursued is present in several international sources. For example, in the Asiatic court-case *Gunarathne vs. Homagama Pradeshiya Sabha et al.* (1998), the Supreme Court makes specific reference to sustainable development, noting that publicity, transparency and fairness are vital if the '*goal*' of sustainable development is to be achieved. The Court explicitly refers to the various components of good governance that are a precondition for sustainable development. Even in the judgement of the Court of Justice of the European Union (September 11th 2012) on the Case C-43/10, sustainable development is defined as a "*target*" enshrined in Article 6 EC. This target is an '*umbrella term*' that encompasses several principles and constitutes a sort of "*process-goal*". Therefore, policy-making was proposed as the thread that

among the fundamental aims of the European Union. The content of the principle substantiates sustainability goals, which conform to weak anthropocentrism and thus to the safeguarding of human health, based on a rational use of resources and aimed at a high level of environmental protection and quality of life[68].

It is useful to remember that the nature of the principle of sustainable development does not seem at all peaceful, because of the vagueness of this concept.

Regardless of the theoretical qualification of this principle, we can certainly believe that it constitutes one of the greatest challenges of humanity in this new millennium. The objectives pointed to by sustainability require an individual commitment, as well as a collective and institutional effort.

Although sustainability law is a suitable tool for resolving conflicts arising from conflicting interests, sometimes, however, one has the impression that the concept of law on the subject of sustainability finds wide applicational difficulties on a practical level. In effect, although many developing countries adhere in principle to the theoretical impositions concerning sustainable development – recognising this notion within their respective constitutions and regulations – they do not draw immediate consequences in practical terms. On the contrary, opposite tendencies emerge from the aims of environmental policies, such as the intensive exploitation of natural resources, the removal of limits that favour the slowing down of development, as well as several protectionist measures towards foreign countries.

3. Sustainability Law and Resilience

The concept of "resilience" finds its own origin in the natural sciences. In effect, ecological resilience was initially conceptualised by Holling as the

---

holds together the components of this development. Sustainable development has been also considered by UNESCO as an "*instrument of policy*", useful to combat climate change. Similarly, the IPCC Fourth Assessment Report (2007) described it as a means able to reduce the vulnerability of climate change, by improving adaptability and increased resistance.

[68] Moreover, European jurisprudence concerning the theme seems to confirm that environmental rules are also authoritative on the subjects of freedom of commerce and competitiveness (European Court of Justice, sentence on "waste oils", case 240/83, February 7th 1985).

capacity of an ecosystem to withstand a disturbance and maintain the same basic processes and structures. He speaks about the capacity for recovery that manifests itself through the combination of perseverance, resistance and transformation (Holling, 1973).

"Sustainable law" has developed to the point of making room for the notion of "resilience", which in fact is progressively emerging. Existential, ethical, ecological, social and economic crises all find a natural response in the ability to resist a negative trend, that is to say through resilience. An 'emergency' dimension, dealing with the study of humanitarian, ethical, environmental, health and social emergencies, is particularly connected to extreme events, catastrophes and more generally to every crisis scenario. In this sense, I have proposed a new branch of sustainability, *Emergency Sustainability*, that aims to overcome the classic bipartition between its 'weak' and 'strong' varieties (Grasso, 2019). The protection of natural resources is increasingly compromised; as is the protection of vulnerable populations who are faced with the consequences of emergencies deriving from climate change and the numerous disasters that often occur unexpectedly as its result. Within this vision, the concept of 'resilience' emerges overwhelmingly. In fact, any emergency presupposes a form of psychological, social, ethical, ecological, anthropological, political or economic resilience.

The link between resilience and sustainability is also particularly evident for other reasons. The failure of legal systems aimed at valuing the resilience of ecosystems, in fact, will probably reduce the sustainability levels of social systems depending in turn on ecosystems. Therefore, in order to move to a sustainability paradigm, human beings should develop a better understanding of resilience, since sustainability[69] depends on social-ecological resilience.

Legal scholars have in the past tended to focus on ecological systems and the law, understood as a social system. More recent contributions relating to law and resilience literature interpret instead a new understanding about resilience, able to realise the system's own capacity to self-organise, adapt and therefore transform (Humby 2014, 104). In this particular sense, Barnes claims that some concepts are essential to understand the meaning of resilience: these concepts are identity, persistence, adaption and transformation, all of which are aspects inherent in the capacity of a system

[69] Sustainability in fact is not a static condition or an end-point, rather it is a dynamic process.

to change when social, economic, political or ecological conditions make the life of the old system unsustainable (Barnes 2016).

The law on sustainability nowadays is increasingly heading towards resilience targets, rather than aims linked to sustainability in a strict sense. The legal and political sources of the entire world recall this expression, and the sustainable development goals essentially go towards the concept of resilience, conceived in its various conceptual declensions.

Within this resilient-sustainable perspective, it is also important to reconcile the rights of nature with human rights, as well as the sphere of development with ongoing emergencies and vulnerabilities. In my opinion, law on the subject of resilience should deal with all of this and can serve as a means of creating a bridge among these issues. This law is a fundamental theoretical matrix to study the different meanings of the sustainability framework.

4. Resilience, Globalisation and Complexity

According to Anthony Giddens, globalisation can be seen as something that we have to learn from and adapt to, because of complexity regarding all social and ecological systems (Giddens, 1990). Resilience could be considered as an answer to globalisation, and as such is particularly influenced by complexity theories that mainly see the world as complex and contingent. The resilience view, thus, suggests a need for people to manifest adaptability and motivational initiative. Jessica Schmidt too refers to an "inner life through learning from exposure to the contingencies of ontological complexity" (Schmidt, 2014; Jonathan 2016, 370-390) while Kai Koddenbrock speaks about a combination of epistemological uncertainty, ontological contingency and relativism (Koddenbrock, 2015, 247).

Kundis Craig distinguishes between 'complex' and 'complicated' systems. According to this perspective, the properties of complex systems include the self-organising nature of the individual components of the system (Craig 2013, 87). Therefore, resilience would not only concern the side of recovering, but it would also be an apparatus constituting social systems.

Moreover, in line with Tracy-Lynn Humby, pluralistic governance is necessary to respond to the 'complexity' of the natural world (Humby, 2014, 130). In this sense, resilience appears to provide a more solid basis to test social limits based on ecological thresholds, considering better complexity about several aspects of society.

Even Barbara Cosens claims that adaptive governance facilitates resilience in social and ecological systems in various ways[70] (Cosens, 2012, 241).

The "complex" and "uncertain" nature of systems leads to a threshold of pessimism concerning the impossibility of doing something in front of catastrophic threats. For this reason, institutions, communities and individuals need to become more 'resilient' and propositive, also increasing their own adaptive capacities in order to respond in a more conscious way to several scenarios. This in truth requires a greater awareness about the adaptation of our own behaviour.

In this regard, resilience is opposed to the disorder emerging in the world and would be able to transform it.

From another point of view, according to Kevin Grove and David Chandler, "If the Anthropocene produces a sense of spatio-temporal disorientation, resilience steadies the ship through a policy of distraction (Taleb, 2012) that naturalises an objectified and future-oriented understanding of time" (Grove and Chandler, 2017).

During the conference organised by the Global Ecological Integrity Group held in 2016 at the philosophy faculty of the University of Munich, I proposed the model of "responsible catastrophism", which I had divided into three theoretical pillars. The third pillar concerned the transformative dimension, where I also showed the concept of *evolutionary/transformative vulnerability*, which is the vulnerability that can evolve and transform itself into resilience; that is to say, a *resilient vulnerability*, which manages to transform its fragility into an opportunity for regeneration. In this sense, we could also speak of *transformative* or *evolutive resilience* (Grasso, 2017).

---

[70] Multiple, overlapping levels of control, horizontal and vertical transfer of information and coordination of decision-making, meaningful public participation, local capacity building, and authority to respond to change in circumstances across a range of scenarios (Cosens, 2012).

5. Theoretical Interpretations About "Resilience Law"

The relationship between resilience and law and, more specifically, law about resilience can be represented by the simple expression: "Resilience Law".

"Resilience Law" is a theoretical formulation that does not technically exist in the literature. A theoretical background on resilience has spread to different disciplines, such as social sciences, humanities and only in small part, to law (Humby, 2014, 85). Most of the "resilience and law" scholarship is concerned with environmental issues and particularly climate topics (Benson 2015, 99; Garmestani et al., 2014; Demange, 2013, 94).

Brand *et al.* distinguish between normative and empirical definitions of resilience. Under the normative interpretation, this concept properly means "flexibility over the long term" (Brand and Jax, 2007, 23).

The notion of "resilience" in a legal context can also be associated with a 'proactive' approach, according to which the law should be applied preventively before things do not function. It in fact is an approach to law, capable of leading towards the future and it individualises useful conditions to identify problems that may arise, while prevention is still feasible. This is an approach deriving from "preventive law"[71] that includes principles aimed at anticipating, but also avoiding, legal issues.

The relationship between law and resilience has also been contemplated by the "Resilience@Law" project which, along with other law firms in Australia, collaborated with the Black Dog Institute in order to make a video series, called "staying well in the law", that deals with the experiences of lawyers regarding their mental wellness[72] (Black Dog Institute, 2016).

The link between law and resilience is equally addressed by a recent theory of so-called "legal resilience", dealing with the resistance of legal

---

[71] Preventive law has its origins in the 1950s, thanks to Professor Louis M. Brown. In the 1980s the National Center for Preventive Law was founded by the California Western School of Law (San Diego). This preventive dimension opposed the typical ex post perspective (dimension of litigations) characterising university education.

[72] The project shows that 33% of lawyers and 20% of barristers suffer disability and distress due to depression. Often they do not seek help and self medicate through alcohol. In effect, alcohol abuse in legal professions is extremely relevant. Moreover, high rates of suicide among lawyers are present. Law students and young lawyers too are most vulnerable to stress effects.

systems to change and their capacity to adapt in response to disturbances, identified as "hybrid threats"[73]. The aim of this theory consists of verifying how legal systems cope with internal and external shocks. In this framework, two different dimensions of legal resilience are identified. The first one concerns the role law is playing to render other social systems more resilient; the second instead deals with the resilience of law itself (Ruhl, 2010, 1375-1378; Sari, 2019).

From this viewpoint, the law does not always obey natural and social systems, as it shows resistance to change[74]. It is also true, as Garmestani et al. argue, that natural systems and their relative forces do not obey the laws of humans (Garmestani et al., 2009, 1036-1054). According to this vision, a certain pragmatic propensity puts too much faith in human capacities to control and manage nature, as well as society. In this sense, legal institutions cannot unilaterally stop hurricanes, prevent droughts, manage sea levels or modify the climate (Garmestani et al., 2014, 4-5).

Current law could certainly be made more flexible to change ecological or social conditions. At the same time, law could facilitate adaptive management, both as a framework for the constitution of laws themselves and as an approach to the management of our natural heritage. Generally, however, the application of resilience theory is problematic, since it is difficult to translate liquid concepts into law, as there are social-ecological resilience elements that are not directly observable (Garmestani et al., 2014, 7).

Resilience can be considered as a possible "antidote" to social vulnerability. For his part, Aguirre argues that the relationship between vulnerability and resilience is a "dialectical unity" (Anguirre 2007, 39). Indeed, vulnerabilities are connected to human, social and ecological impotence and constitute an opportunity for improving resilience and adaptive capacity. However, as Humby recalls, efforts at mitigating risks are based on an incomplete knowledge and the creation of new unexpected vulnerabilities that lead to building a temporary adaptation (Humby, 2014).

---

[73] NATO and the EU have embraced the concept of "hybrid welfare" to describe the threats. According to the theory of legal resilience, the concepts of hybrid welfare, gray zone conflict and lawfare lack precision and they may be under and over inclusive.

[74] The rigidity of our current legal framework in fact is not well suited to the complexity of social-ecological systems.

6. Use of the Word "Resilience" in Several Sources

Various political-legal documents (or soft-law sources) contemplate the concept of resilience. For example, worthy of mention is the "Opinion of the European Economic and Social Committee" on 'Resilient democracy through a strong and diverse civil society' (2019/C 228/04), which describes the features of a "resilient democracy". Similarly, the Joint Communication to the European Parliament, the European Council, and the Council "Increasing resilience and bolstering capabilities to address hybrid threats" [JOIN (2018) 16 final] are essential in order to understand the concept of 'hybrid threats', constituting one of various theoretical assumptions regarding a resilience framework.

We should also recall Regulation (EU) No 375/2014 of the European Parliament and of the Council establishing the European Voluntary Humanitarian Aid Corps ('EU Aid Volunteers initiative'), as well as Regulation (EU) No 233/2014 of the European Parliament and of the Council on a financing instrument relating to development cooperation for the period 2014-2020.

The notion of resilience is even included in the "American Presidential Policy Directive on Critical Infrastructure Security and Resilience" (2013) and it is described as the ability to prepare for and adapt to changing conditions, withstanding and recovering from every form of disruption.

The key points relating to the European resilience plan (2021) are: green transition; digital transformation; smart, sustainable and inclusive growth; social and territorial cohesion; and health, economic, social and institutional resilience. According to the definition of resilience that emerges from the document drawn up by the European Commission on recovery and resilience[75], "resilience" means: "the ability to face economic, social and environmental shocks and/or structural changes in a fair, sustainable and inclusive way. The COVID-19 crisis has put to the test the capacity of Member States and the Union to cope with large and unexpected shocks, including vulnerabilities of health systems to cope with high contagion rates, disruptions in demand and supply, or other underlying structural weaknesses to their accessibility, effectiveness and resilience"[76].

---

[75] European Commission. 2021. Commission Staff Working Document Guidance to Member States Recovery and Resilience Plans, 22.01.2021, SWD (2021) 12 final, Brussels.

[76] *Ibidem* (page 6).

One of the topics where the concept of resilience is mostly used is in relation to climate change[77] and disaster management, as well as pandemic frameworks. Below, I will be showing the application of this concept to some climate and disaster sources.

7. Resilience, Climate Change, Disaster Law and Governance

The resilience topic particularly emerges in some cases on climate change. For instance, in the legal case "Rosado v. Pruitt" (2018), the plaintiffs mentioned the need to carry out coastal resilience projects, due to sea level rise[78]. Also in the "Clement v. U.S. Department of Interior" case (2017), native Alaska communities, with regard to climate threats, referred to opportunities for developing resilience plans[79].

Furthermore, the Petition of Torres Strait Islanders to the United Nations Human Rights Committee (2019), alleging violations stemming from Australia's inaction on climate change, is very clear in this sense. Eight Torres Strait Islanders, in fact, submitted a petition to the United Nations Human Rights Committee against the Australian government, asserting that its omissions with regard to climate change – and particularly insufficient and inadequate mitigation plans and resilience measures on the islands, such as e.g. seawalls[80] – were violating the fundamental human rights of Australians[81].

---

[77] In the Glossary of the last IPCC report (Annex II), resilience is defined as the capacity of social, economic and environmental systems to cope with a hazardous event, trend, or disturbance, by responding or reorganising in ways that maintain their essential function, identity and structure, while also maintaining the capacity for adaptation, learning and transformation.

[78] United States District Court Eastern District of New York, Rosado vs. Pruitt, Memorandum and Order, 17-Cv-4843 (Erk), 2018.

[79] Also in the case "Bard Campaign v. Secretary of State for Communities and Local Government" (2019), some locations proposed as 'ecotowns' are criticised in respect to best practices in urban sustainability and climate change resilience. See: High Court of Justice, Queen's Bench Division, "Bard Campaign vs. Secretary of State for Communities and Local Government" (2019).

[80] United Nations Human Rights Committee. 2019. Petition of Torres Strait Islanders to the United Nations Human Rights Committee.

[81] This petition represents the first legal action in Australia concerning a violation of human rights because of climate change.

Among the soft law sources on climate change and disasters, including the resilience branch, I would particularly mention the Paris Agreement and the Sendai Framework. The Paris Agreement on climate change (2015), in fact, intends to reduce greenhouse gas emissions in order to restrain the global temperature increase well below 2°C compared to pre-industrial levels, continuing efforts to limit it to 1.5 °C. The agreement, therefore, requires a greater commitment aimed at achieving a better level of climate resilience and adaptation to the impacts caused by climate change.

The Sendai Framework for Disaster Risk Reduction (2015-2030), instead, identifies climate change and variability as the most important factors leading to disaster, together with uncontrolled urbanisation[82] and poor land management[83]. This tool is aimed at improving a coherence link between climate change policies and agri-environmental, social and health policies[84]. The European action plan relating to this framework has therefore recognised the reduction of the risk of disasters as a useful opportunity to strengthen the resilience of the European Union with respect to the harmful effects caused by the climate. This policy focuses on the adoption of measures that address the three dimensions of disaster risk (exposure to hazards, vulnerabilities together with capabilities and ultimately risk characteristics), in order to prevent the creation of new risks, reduce existing risks and increase resilience to resisting residual risk[85].

In February 2017, the United Nations General Assembly approved the recommendations of the Intergovernmental Working Group of Experts working on indicators related to disaster risk reduction, thanks to a Resolution of the General Assembly (A/RES/71/276). The adoption of 38 global indicators[86] able to measure progress against the achievement of the

---

[82] Conscious urban planning plays a significant role in increasing climate resilience, particularly in densely populated coasts and river basins.

[83] UNISDR. 2015. Sendai Framework for Disaster Risk Reduction 2015–2030.

[84] Furthermore, the EU civil protection mechanism requires the various member countries to conduct appropriate multi-risk assessments.

[85] In the field of disasters the term resilience can be found in some documents, such as: the European Parliament Resolution on the EU approach to resilience and disaster risk reduction in developing countries: learning from food security crises [2013/2110 (INI)]; or the Ethical Principles on Disaster Risk Reduction and People's Resilience to Disasters (Council of Europe, AP/CAT (2011) 02 Rev. 2).

[86] The list of indicators can be found on the site: https://www.preventionweb.net/drr-framework/sendai-framework-monitor/indicators

7 objectives[87] of the Sendai Framework will allow Member States and the global community to systematically monitor progress in preventing new risks and reducing existing risks, as well as to strengthen the resilience of various communities. Ultimately, the indicators will have to provide useful tools to guarantee a precise responsibility.

With these indicators, UNISDR began the development of a prototype of the Sendai Framework Monitoring System. It is a global online tool, established on March 1, 2018, which allows countries to report and monitor progress on the implementation of the 7 objectives. The system allows countries to align their relationships with their respective national strategies and plans. Given that each country faces challenges that are linked to its territory through personalised responses, UNISDR also supports the development of customised indicators, in order to allow the countries involved to measure the progress made at the national level under the framework of Sendai[88].

The 2013 European Climate Change Adaptation Strategy (COM/2013/0216 final) also aims to make Europe more climate resilient and to this end identifies 8 specific actions[89]. This strategy seeks to help Member States to adapt to the current and future impacts of climate change, improving national adaptation strategies, increasing and perfecting the sharing of knowledge on the subject, and implementing adequate integration between

---

[87] In summary, the seven objectives, to be pursued by 2030, concern: (1) the substantial reduction in world mortality caused by catastrophes; (2) the substantial reduction in the number of people affected; (3) the reduction of economic losses in relation to world GDP; (4) the substantial reduction of damage caused by disasters to critical infrastructures; (5) the increase in the number of countries with national and local strategies to reduce catastrophe risks (by 2020); (6) strengthening international cooperation; and (7) increased availability and access to multi-risk early warning systems and disaster risk assessments.

[88] UNISDR, Annual Report 2017, 2016-17 Biennium Work Programme Final Report, Ginevra, United Nations, 2018.

[89] Action 1: encourage all Member States to adopt global adaptation strategies; Action 2: provide funding through the LIFE program to support capacity building and strengthen adaptation actions in Europe (2014-2020); Action 3: include adaptation within the framework of the Covenant of Mayors (2013/2014); Action 4: remedy the lack of knowledge; Action 5: further develop the Climate-ADAPT platform as a "one-stop shop" for information on adaptation in Europe; Action 6: promote the acquisition of "environmentally proof" features of the common agricultural policy, the cohesion policy and the common fisheries policy; Action 7: ensure a more resilient infrastructure; and Action 8: promote insurance and other financial products to facilitate resilient investment and commercial decisions.

the different policy sectors. Between 2013 and 2018, the number of European States with a national adaptation strategy has increased from 15 to 25[90].

Unlike the Sustainable Development Goals, for which shareable indicators have been identified, the global climate resilience goal has yet to be effectively implemented. The ongoing revision of the national adaptation plans, aimed at assessing the progress made, will in fact lead to a first realistic nucleus of results in only a few years[91].

The European Commission's recent report on the implementation of the European climate change adaptation strategy of 12 November 2018 [COM (2018) 738 final] shows that the strategy in question, despite having promoted adaptation plans at all levels, has proved less effective in the implementation and monitoring phase of the same plans[92]. With regard to the number of local adaptation strategies, some progress was slower than expected in 2013, and these varied among Member States. For the future, the strategy aims to achieve better results related to disaster risk reduction, especially with regard to the integration of adaptation in specific methodologies and indicators, and to the promotion of social vulnerability assessment[94].

The strengthening of climate change resilience is also pursued through a multilevel analysis of vulnerabilities concerning territories and communities. In Europe, for example, a national multi-sectoral assessment of the impacts of climate change, vulnerabilities and related risks has been made by most European countries[95]. The study of vulnerabilities is a fundamental prerequisite for being able to predispose resilient actions that

---

[90] European Commission. 2018. Report from the Commission to the European Parliament and the Council, COM (2018) 738 final on the implementation of the EU Strategy on adaptation to climate change.

[91] European Commission. 2017. Study to Support the Evaluation of the EU Adaptation Strategy. Brussels.

[92] European Commission. 2018. Evaluation of the EU on adaptation to climate change, 12.11.2018, SWD (2018) 461 final. Brussels.

[94] European Commission. 2018. Evaluation of the EU on adaptation to climate change, 12.11.2018, SWD (2018) 461 final, Brussels.

[95] Both climate change adaptation and disaster risk reduction are integrated tools in the main European policies and strategies, including those for critical infrastructure protection, environmental protection, cohesion policy financial instruments and structural and investment funds, agriculture, nutrition, nutritional security and integrated management costs.

counteract climate change. Nevertheless, it must be noted that these evaluations were carried out in very different periods, without a homogeneous temporal coordination.

8. Some Tipping Points

Although within the framework of national climate change adaptation plans many governments[96] are committed to integrating considerations on adaptation in development plans and sectoral strategies[97], some tipping points concerning resilience and climate change issues will be shown in the next sections.

8.1. Tipping Points on "Mainstreaming"

Mainstreaming policies[98] have been slow to translate into solid field actions. Although, in fact, the adoption of instruments suitable for the assessment of vulnerabilities is increasing internationally, only a few governments use all possible supplementary options. The European Commission itself notes the actions envisaged by the adaptation strategy

---

[96] For example, the German strategy for adapting to climate change has given rise to the mainstreaming platform, in order to increase institutional capacity.

[97] UNFCCC. 2016. Aggregate Effect of the Intended Nationally Determined Contributions: An Update, UN Doc FCCC/CP/2016/2.

[98] "Mainstreaming" (i.e., the integration process) concerning the integration of adaptation into the various European policies was and remains one of the pillars of the 2009 European Commission White Paper "Adapting to climate change: towards a European framework for action" and continues to be an important goal for the 2013 European adaptation strategy. Furthermore, the framework established by the seventh environmental action program "Living well, within the limits of our planet" also refers to the integration of adaptation into other policy areas of the Union.

Integration is an iterative process that requires a multi-level assessment concerning the national, sub-national and local spheres, and should be capable of involving a variety of governmental and non-governmental actors. This assessment concerns climatic information, the risks linked to the sectoral objectives, and the strategies aimed at reducing these risks, and it is also proposed to reduce the vulnerabilities and increase the appropriate efforts to build adaptive capacity. It can determine some changes to the sectoral objectives and, more generally, aid with a cultural change in the daily decision-making processes of the various institutions involved. The integration of adaptation to climate change in the sectoral policies of the EU particularly concerns water policies (relating to inland waters, such as rivers and lakes), forestry, agriculture, biodiversity infrastructure and migration. Integration is an essential component of an adequate global adaptation policy.

could be better integrated with each other[99]. A review of over 100 cases related to integration efforts found that although the vast majority of the countries involved (developed and developing countries) have channelled mainstreaming into documents and sectoral policy plans, only half of them have really proposed projects and concrete activities (Runhaar, 2017, 1201-1210).

The Intergovernmental Panel on Climate Change (IPCC) also acknowledges in the "Fifth Assessment Report" that integration has been implemented in a limited way, despite the extensive documentation of the plans at national, sub-national and community level. Several factors contribute to this shortcoming (Bouyé et al., 2018). First, mainstreaming efforts involve a wide range of actors, institutions and processes. Consequently, the transition from planning to implementation requires the overcoming of many barriers, which according to Gogoi et al. concerns resources, institutions and capacities (Gogoi et al., 2017).

The obstacles to implementation include the lack of a serious and constant political commitment, the lack of cooperation between the main parties involved, and conflicting political interests.

Even Bouye et al., for example, conclude that the integration process requires greater attention to the link between the different institutional, political and financial instruments, as well as constant monitoring to support implementation (Bouyé et al., 2018).

8.2. Tipping Points on Climate Change and Human Health

Global warming has and will have increasingly devastating effects on people's health and humanitarian crises: water scarcity, increase in diarrheal diseases linked to drought, food insecurity, population displacements, natural disasters, and spread of infectious diseases linked to the replication of new vectors, amongst other things. Since the 1980s, each successive decade has been warmer than all previous ones since the 1850s, while Arctic ice is shrinking at a rate of about 13 percent (per decade). The 2003 heat

---

[99] European Commission. 2018. Report from the Commission to the European Parliament and the Council, COM (2018) 738 final. For example, Climate-ADAPT could provide a more detailed overview of current research projects on climate change or other EU-funded activities. Furthermore, the renewed European civil protection mechanism should promote better connections between adaptation and disaster risk reduction.

wave caused more than 70,000 deaths in 12 European countries. Heat waves are expected to cause more than 120,000 deaths a year in the European Union by 2050. Over 220 million new exposures were calculated in 2018 compared to the 1986-2005 period. High temperatures can cause respiratory and cardiovascular problems, especially among children and the elderly, and lead to premature deaths. These temperatures favour forest fires and help to extend the areas where disease-carrying insects (such as ticks and mosquitoes) survive and multiply. These insects can cause health issues such as Lyme disease, dengue fever and malaria. Climate change will also affect biodiversity and food production capacity, contributing to the risk of malnutrition and rising food prices on a global scale. Vector capacity for malaria transmission has increased by more than 20% in Africa since 1950 and the WHO predicts further major future increases in malaria mortality in central and eastern sub-Saharan Africa. The pathologies caused by climate change are among the most varied, such as Dengue, Chikungunya, Zika, and Congo-Crimean fevers. Devastating floods will be increasingly frequent, while drought will determine the risk of new war scenarios for water. The Inuit petition and the legal case of the island of Kivalina relate to the violation of the rights about which the respective inhabitants complain, including the right to health (Grasso, 2012).

Before examining some tipping points in this context, I would like to underline some issues. The ability of health systems to respond to climate change varies greatly between different European countries. This variation certainly reflects historical processes and current economic constraints, but it is also the global symptom of a poor awareness of the problem, which in turn generates inevitable political omissions.

In this regard, the World Health Organization highlights the omissions of European countries regarding the integration between health policies and climate change adaptation measures. Very few countries, in fact, would have developed national or subnational programmes for health adaptation[100].

As we unfortunately learn from the work of the World Health Organization Regional Office for Europe (2017), health resilience, compared to specific climate change adaptation plans, is decidedly scarce. Even when some countries show a serious desire to integrate the sphere of health with

[100] World Health Organization Regional Office for Europe. 2017. Protecting health in Europe from Climate Change, Copenhagen.

that of adaptation to the climate, we soon realise that the scheduling times are definitely extended over time[101].

8.3. Tipping Points on Climate Change and Adaptation

The ongoing revision of the national adaptation plans, aimed at assessing the progress made, will in fact lead to a first realistic nucleus of results only in a few years' time[102].

The Commission's recent report on the implementation of the European climate change adaptation strategy of 12 November 2018 [COM (2018) 738 final] shows that the strategy in question, despite having promoted adaptation plans at all levels, has proved to be less than effective in their implementation and monitoring. The slowness with which adaptation policies are developed contrasts with the speed at which the disastrous effects of climate change manifest themselves[103].

By 2017 only 15 Member States had developed a national adaptation plan[104]. Between 2013 and 2018, the number of Member States with a national adaptation strategy increased from 15 to 25[105]. As of 2017 there were 28 European countries (25 EU Member States and 3 member countries of the European Environment Agency)[106] which had adopted a national adaptation strategy, while only 17 countries (i.e., 15 EU Member States and 2 EEA member countries) had developed a national adaptation plan. Among the latter, only a few States have detailed action plans, which contain real programmatic approaches[107].

---

[101] *Ibidem*. In this regard, in the very recent UK Report on the "Third Strategy on adaptation to climate change" (Department of Environment Food & Rural Affairs, 2018) it is stated that the health sector intends to incorporate adaptation into daily practice. However, this would only occur by 2023.

[102] European Commission. 2017. Study to Support the Evaluation of the EU Adaptation Strategy, Brussels.

[103] European Commission. 2018. Report from the Commission to the European Parliament and the Council, COM (2018) 738 final.

[104] European Environment Agency. 2018. National Climate Change Vulnerability and Risk Assessments in Europe 2018, EEA Report No 1/2018.

[105] European Commission. 2018. Report from the Commission to the European Parliament and the Council, COM (2018) 738 final.

[106] EEA is the abbreviation of "European Environment Agency".

[107] Among these States is Denmark, which in 2011 approved an action plan mainly concerning water management in cases of extreme events.

Furthermore, on 23 February 2016, the European Environment Agency sent a short questionnaire to all its 33 member countries, as well as 6 cooperating countries[108]. Responses were only been received from 22 countries[109]. Among those that did not provide any feedback we find Spain and Great Britain[110].

After the publication of the European report on climate change adaptation platforms in Europe, the number of adaptation platforms in EEA member countries increased from 14 to 16 in 2017, while further platforms are still being prepared and/or are under refinement[111].

Generally and at present, most European countries have adopted an adaptation strategy, with the exception of Bulgaria, Croatia, Iceland, Latvia and Liechtenstein. However, as already mentioned, a specific national adaptation plan has only been adopted by 17 countries. Furthermore, among the 24 countries that responded to the survey, only 8 stated that their plan was integrated with the national adaptation strategy, while 7 countries confirmed that this plan was separate from the strategy[112].

The degree of climate resilience also contrasts through a multilevel analysis of vulnerabilities related to a territory or a community. These multi-level assessments were carried out in the various countries with uneven timing between them. The last assessment made by Spain, for example, dates back to 2005, while the most recent evaluations refer to 2017 (such as the UK assessment).

---

[108] The European Environment Agency has 6 cooperating countries: Albania, Bosnia and Herzegovina, the Yugoslav Republic of Macedonia, Montenegro, Serbia and Kosovo.

[109] The countries that answered the questionnaire are: Austria, Belgium, Bulgaria, Croatia, Estonia, Finland, France, Germany, Hungary, Ireland, Italy, Lithuania, Malta, the Netherlands, Poland, Portugal, Romania and Sweden, along with Liechtenstein, Norway, Switzerland and Turkey.

[110] The countries that did not answer the questionnaire are: the United Kingdom, Spain, Cyprus, Czech Republic, Denmark, Greece, Iceland, Latvia, Luxembourg, Slovakia, and Slovenia.

[111] EEA. 2015. *Overview of Climate Change Adaptation Platforms in Europe*, EEA Technical Report No 5/2015, European Environment Agency.

[112] EEA. 2018. *National Climate Change Vulnerability and Risk Assessments in Europe 2018*, EEA Report No 1/2018, European Environment Agency.

8.4. Tipping Points on Climate Refugees

In the light of the United Nations Convention on the Status of Refugees (signed in Geneva on July 28, 1951), a refugee is someone who – rightly fearing of being persecuted for reasons of race, religion, nationality, membership to a particular social group or for their political opinions – is outside the country of which they are a citizen and cannot or does not want, because of this fear, to avail themself of the protection of this country. Or a refugee can be understood as someone who, not having a citizenship and being outside the country in which they had their habitual residence, cannot or does not want to return there due to the aforementioned fears.

The expression "internally displaced person", on the other hand, refers to someone who for similar reasons has been forced to flee, while remaining within the territory of their own country.

The First Protocol to the Geneva Conventions of 12 August 1949, adopted in June 1977 in Geneva and entered into force on 7 December 1978, relating to the protection of victims of international armed conflicts, considers environmental protection only in the context of war situations (Article 55 of the Protocol).

Therefore, the Geneva Convention (1951) does not recognise the figure of the "climate refugee", because it does not recognise the environment as a cause of "persecution". Among the asylum seekers who do not fall within the definition of the Geneva Convention, therefore, there are also environmental refugees – fleeing from environmental disasters – to which the High Commissioner offers primary assistance for humanitarian reasons.

The *Handbook on Procedures and Criteria for Determining Refugee Status*, which is undoubtedly the most authoritative interpretation of the 1951 Refugee Convention and thus of the Protocol to the Refugee Convention (1967), states that there is no universally accepted definition of persecution and various attempts to formulate this definition have met with little success (see: Westra, 2021; Westra, Satvinder and Scovazzi, 2015).

No possible interpretation of international sources on the subject can take into consideration the category of migrations determined by environmental reasons.

There are also those who have proposed to implement a new Convention aimed at protecting the rights of environmental refugees (Grasso, 2015). Indeed, existing rights should be reinterpreted in the context of environmental concerns, which were not important when these rights were first formulated.

The Nansen Conference on Climate Change and Displacement (Norway, June 2011) identifies ten principles on "climate change and transboundary displaced persons", which reaffirm the role of civil society, regional integration processes and international cooperation.

The conference held in Geneva on the occasion of the annual International Dialogue on Migration (2011) – promoted by the International Organization for Migration and entitled "Climate change, environmental degradation and migration" – identified three areas within which to call upon institutions to strengthen their management skills with reference to the relationship between climate change and migration. These areas concern: 1. the creation of knowledge on the subject and the improvement of data collection through the study of the relationships between the various factors that distinguish migration; 2. the consolidation of the legal, political and institutional framework through the harmonisation and flexibility of existing regulations, as well as the improvement of cooperation between the various levels (local, national and supranational); and 3. the development of technical and political capacities (including management and prevention).

On December 17, 2018, the United Nations General Assembly affirmed the Global Compact on Refugees. However, the state of climate refugees was not recognised in this source either.

Two hundred million climate migrants are estimated by 2050; in 2019 alone, according to the Internal Displacement Monitoring Center, 17.2 million people were forced to flee due to destructive phenomena and weather hazards. The United Nations Environment Program (UNEP) estimates the number of climate refugees in Africa alone is expected to reach fifty million by 2060 (Grasso, 2015).

Displacement represents a last resort solution that must be implemented on a voluntary basis (i.e., people in identified communities must be free to refuse participation in programmes) based on careful planning. There is a need for accurate assessment of the socio-economic, demographic and environmental situation, consultations with local communities and national authorities, and fruitful assistance systems.

In addition to the requirement of voluntariness, the limits of the displacement also concern paradoxical situations: for example, many of the displaced people whose fate was determined after the floods that occurred in the area of the Zambezi River, had to temporarily return to their homes, cultivating their respective fields, since it was the only way to support themselves. We should consider also that some migrants were transferred to Mozambique and placed in arid areas where a condition of serious drought was a burden (Grasso, 2015).

8.5. Tipping Points on Climate Insurance

If for example we think only of Action n. 7 of the European Climate Change Adaptation Strategy [113], which is aimed at ensuring more resilient infrastructures, the existing standards on the subject have been selected and subjected to a review that began in 2017. Action 8 wants to promote the insurance instrument and other financial products for resilient investments[114]. The European revision speaks in this case of "equivocal evidence", due to an insufficient use of this instrument. In general, the initiated strategic review indicates the need for greater collective action on resilience[115].

The "Green Paper on Disaster Insurance" (natural and man-made), which was drafted by the European Commission in 2013, emphasised the role of insurance schemes related to extreme climate scenarios.

Insurance is the risk transfer concerning a loss going from one individual to another in exchange for a fee, that is to say a premium. Climate insurance concerns insurance against certain extreme weather events (such as droughts, floods or hurricanes) and related phenomena (sea level rise, desertification, crop failure and so on).

Analytical research undertaken by the EU Joint Research Centre shows that there is currently a low market penetration rate of disaster insurance in certain Member States[116].

---

[113] European Commission. 2013. European Climate Change Adaptation Strategy: COM /2013/0216 final.
[114] The "Green Paper on Disaster Insurance" (natural and man-made), which was drafted by the European Commission in 2013, emphasised the role of insurance schemes related to extreme climate scenarios. Unfortunately, however, the insurance instrument has unfortunately been considered an alternative solution to adaptation.
[115] This is so despite the fact that some states have equipped themselves with efficient national resilience centres, such as Scotland.
[116] Joint Research Centre. 2012. European Commission, Natural Catastrophes: Risk Relevance and Insurance Coverage in the EU.

Although overall there is no lack of best practices on climate insurance, as in the United Kingdom, France and Denmark[117], the main tipping points concerning this instrument are mentioned below.

The first tipping point relating to this tool refers to a certain ambiguity that characterises the original meaning of the term "insurance" in the field of climate change issues. The members of the Alliance of Small Island States, who first introduced the term 'insurance' in the climate debate, were not asking for insurance as such. Rather, they were asking for aid, even in the form of compensation. Therefore, in asking for funds useful to cover losses associated with the highest probability of sea-level rise, in reality they were not asking for insurance.

Nevertheless, the notion of insurance in this framework can be justified due to strategic incentives addressed to employ the concept of insurance. In effect, there is a markable difference between "insurance" and "aid". This last term in fact could connote arbitrariness or inadequacy. The term "insurance", conversely, would concern individuals adopting a system of mutual compensation.

From a semantic viewpoint, according to Göran Duus-Otterström and Sverker C. Jagers, the notion of insurance might be an "easier sell to the main generic burden carriers" (Duus-Otterström and Jagers, 2011, 334), such as the developed countries that are particularly exposed to demands for adaptation because of their important historical responsibility and large wealth (Duus-Otterström and Jagers, 2011, 334).

From an ethical perspective, the risk is that most vulnerable countries (i.e., those with the greatest need of being insured) will not be able to afford it. Their vulnerability would translate into excessive premiums. Furthermore, from a merely economic perspective, insuring the most vulnerable would not be very convenient.

The second tipping point mainly concerns uncertainty about future climatic impacts. In effect, there is a disagreement on how future impacts should be modelled. For instance, indirect impacts are more difficult to be estimated in monetary terms, even if some efforts useful in order to adopt these impacts do exist in some models (Hudson et al., 2017, 179-208).

---

117 European Commission. 2018. Using insurance in adaptation to climate change. Luxembourg: Publications Office of the European Union.

The uncertainty regarding future impacts might generate costs in excess, the covering of which would mean that commercial insurance is always a bad bet for risk-neutral agents (Gardiner, 2006).

Furthermore, as the European Commission shows, changes in vulnerability are often modelled as exogenous changes, taking place at a single time, rather than as adaptive behaviour that occurs when risk develops[118]. As Richard S. J. Tol recalled, the option of insuring climate change is limited because the associated damages are hardly quantifiable and not particularly diversifiable (Tol, 1998).

The third tipping point concerns the inhomogeneity characterising political evaluations of the vulnerability of different countries. The vulnerabilities related to climate change are different from one country to another, and even the studies related to them can diversify, since the criteria to determine and assess a certain threshold of vulnerability may not be homogeneous among different countries. Indeed the lack of homogeneity is not limited to the criteria in question, but also concerns the timing with which assessments are made on the various vulnerabilities. For example, in Europe, assessments on the state of climate change impacts, vulnerabilities and consequent risks have been carried out in various countries at very different times[119].

A further critical aspect concerns the scarce use of the insurance instrument with respect to climate change. In this regard, the European revision of adaptation plans[120] speaks of "equivocal evidence" due to insufficient use of this tool. Furthermore, the European Union has recently extended some recommendations to the Member States. One in particular concerns the need for European countries to assess their vulnerability in relation to insurance penetration rates and covered events, reporting on how

[118] European Commission, August 2017, Insurance of weather and climate related disaster risk: Inventory and analysis of mechanisms to support damage prevention in the EU, Luxembourg: Publications Office of the European Union, 2017.

[119] EEA. 2018. National Climate Change Vulnerability and Risk Assessments in Europe, EEA Report No 1/2018, European Environment Agency. The last assessment made by Spain, for example, dates back to 2005, while the most recent evaluations refer to 2017 (such as the UK assessment).

[120] The ongoing review of national adaptation plans includes an assessment of progress made although it will lead to a reliable core of results in the near future (European Commission. 2017. Study to Support the Evaluation of the EU Adaptation Strategy. Brussels).

they use insurance as a mechanism for managing risks[121]. It includes an *ex-ante* conditionality on assessing insurance vulnerability[122].

Another tipping-point in this framework relates to the fact that the most vulnerable countries would face comparatively high premiums, which they presumably would not be able to afford. Indeed, some regions may be 'uninsurable'. Developed countries, which are characterised by low probability, have few incentives to belong to a common insurance pool. If they choose to take part, their premiums will be comparatively low. This means that the insurance scheme might have too little funding to cover some damages.

Therefore, an insurance model does not necessarily equate to some form of justice. The IPCC report concludes that insurance can be a useful tool for risk reduction, but also warns that this tool could discourage such reduction if it is not correctly organised.

A further tipping point is linked to risk and low probability scenarios. Insurers indemnify against some catastrophic losses, though we should underline that not all risks are necessarily catastrophic (Bougen, 2003).

There are cases, then, where disaster insurance markets do not appear to deal entirely with existing risks. For instance, penetration rates are high in most European States. In relation to floods and earthquakes, however, penetration rates are only high in cases where those risks are valued with other risks.

Generally, a risk is endogenous if the person who is at risk has a certain level of control over the damage (Tol, 1998, 258). In the case of climate change, however, endogeneity of risk is limited by the character of low probability that the potential hazardous event actually will occur.

With regard to low probability and serious consequence events, policy-makers will question – after the hazardous event – what they could have done but didn't in terms of prevention and preparation. If the degree of

[121] European Commission. 2017. Insurance of weather and climate related disaster risk: Inventory and analysis of mechanisms to support damage prevention in the EU. Luxembourg: Publications Office of the European Union.

[122] The European Commission's Sendai Action Plan promotes the consideration of disaster resilience and risk prevention and management in implementation of the European Structural and Investment Funds programmes.

prevention neglected increases, the social vulnerability obviously becomes more sensitive.

Low probability risks are especially controversial because experts often disagree about the chances and potential effects associated with specific events. Many policy problems arise when people ignore risks characterised by low probabilities. Individuals, in fact, seem to buy insurance only when the probability of risk is above a given threshold, even when insurance is heavily subsidised against a loss (Slovic et al., 1977). People tend to view insurance as an investment, rather than as a protection against loss. According to Slovic, a series of laboratory studies of insurance decision-making would show that people buy more insurance against events with a high probability of inflicting a relatively small loss than low-probability, high-loss events (Slovic et al., 1977). This would call into question the "Utility Theory of Insurance"[123].

Moreover, as the "Green Paper on the insurance of natural and man-made disasters" recalls, consumers may not be inclined to insure themselves against risks that are unlikely to individually impact on them, underestimating the real risk of a disaster ("myopia risk")[124].

One final tipping point concerns the category of maladaptation, i.e., an incorrect form of adaptation. The Alliance of Small Island States proposed in 1991 the creation of an international insurance device in order to compensate damages from sea level rise. UNFCCC mentions insurance as an adaptation tool (Article 4.8) and Article 3.14 of the Kyoto Protocol also recalls insurance as a climate change response, as does the Bali Action Plan of 2007.

Insurance as an instrument was wrongly considered a form of adaptation, as was displacement (in the case of climate refugees). In my opinion, these two realities (insurance and displacement) are rather forms of maladaptation, or at least a limiting adaptation. Insurance does not in fact create an adaptive process in the truest sense of the term and displacement, rather than being a form of adaptation, is instead the failure of climate

---

[123] This theory has been proposed both as a prescriptive model, as it proposes when insurance should be purchased, but also as a descriptive model, as it is indicating how insurance decisions are made.

[124] European Commission. 2013. "Green Paper on the insurance of natural and man-made disasters", COM (2013) 213 final.

policies which, in light of the various omissions, force some of the most vulnerable populations to new housing settlements.

According to Paul O'Hare, Iain White, and Angela Connelly, insurance catalyses a cycle of maladaptation, promoting a rapid recovery, without however encouraging an adaptation process and therefore reinforcing societal risks. Insurance promotes resilience through the spreading of responsibility, abating however the incentive to action (O'Hare et al., 2015).

9. Climate Change, Resilience and the Local Dimension

The concept of resilience has spread in a way that affects cities all over the world. During the climate summit organised by local and regional leaders at the 23rd United Nations Conference on climate change (2017), cities and regions expressed an interest in the topic in question, undersigning the Bonn-Fiji commitment. In February 2018, the World Urban Forum launched the Dialogue of Cities and Regions, which invited local and sub-national governments to participate in the decision-making process related to climate action. The IPCC Conference for Cities and Climate, held in Edmonton (Canada) in March 2018, considered the state of academic knowledge by establishing a joint research programme at the global level. During this event, the first series of *Talanoa Dialogues of Cities and Regions* was announced and developed by the Congress "Resilient Cities 2018", which was held in Bonn (Germany) in April 2018, in addition to the ICLEI World Congress realised in Montréal in June of the same year. At COP23, ICLEI and the Global Island Partnerships also established the "Frontline Cities and Islands", a movement of mayors and leaders of economies committed to promoting local action and to providing resilient integrated solutions. Currently, through the Frontline initiative, ICLEI and the aforementioned Partnerships support the strengthening of local government for resilience, providing useful tools for disaster risk reduction and supporting local governments to develop joint work programmes[125].

Among the networks of cities dealing with the issue of climate change resilience, some emerge particularly well. The Covenant of Mayors for Climate and Energy, for example, brings together local and regional authorities which voluntarily undertake the implementation of the EU's energy mitigation, adaptation and sustainability objectives on their

---

[125] ICLEI. 2018. Resilient Cities Report 2018: Tracking local progress on the resilience targets of SDG 11, Bonn.

territory[126]. A more global version of the previous network was created in 2016 with the Global Covenant of Mayors for Climate and Energy. This network aims to become the largest global coalition committed to climate leadership at the local level. It can enable comparisons between cities and regions around the world, in order to combat climate change and promote local climate resilience[127].

Even the City Resilience Campaign promoted by UNISDR works for sustainable urbanisation and addresses issues of local governance and urban risk. It aims to improve the degree of resilience between local governments and urban communities around the world. The network "100 Resilient Cities" deserves special attention, as it is aimed at helping cities around the world to become more resistant to physical, social and economic challenges[128].

10. Line of Analysis

Regarding the topic of resilience, the role of law compared to that of policy is rather marginal. Despite this, it cannot be ignored that this topic has entered the legal sphere. However, the concept of resilience today is more assimilable to the legal and political literature on climate change and disasters.

In my opinion, therefore, it would be preferable to speak of "Resilience Law", intending with this expression a meta-legal branch that proposes a scientific knowledge about the evolution concerning the relationship between resilience and law. As a branch it stands out for its strategic capacity to counteract the real threats characterising this millennium, that is to say threats deriving from disaster scenarios, which are mainly determined by growing climate change. Precisely because of its meta-nature and considering its importance in front of institutional omissions both locally and globally, I would like to define this law as a law which has the formal structure of "justice".

Below I will try to explain the emergency dimension of this vision of a new law, through the application of some basic theories on legal change.

---

[126] https://www.covenantofmayors.eu/en/
[127] https://www.globalcovenantofmayors.org
[128] https://www.100resilientcities.org

Through some study hypotheses, thus, I will be illustrating four possible theoretical frameworks of change, which will try to interpret Resilience Law according to certain classifications: the first two categories examine this particular law in accordance with the theories of change suggested by Friedman and Luhmann. The third, in turn, supposes a sociocultural evolution, while the final one sees change from the perspectives of transfer, spread, transmission, imitation, transplant, convergence, circulation, borrowing, globalisation, and diffusion or better "interaction".

11. Changes in Law: Theoretical References

First of all, let us examine what is intended by "change in law". Juridical change regards dynamic interaction of the law with other areas of human action: compared to society, in effect, the law can be intended both in terms of a dependent variable and an independent variable. Without neglecting Bentham and Savigny, who historically represent these two antithetical methods of viewing law within society[129], we should remember, for instance, the research carried out by Adam Podgórecki on "Social Engineering"[130], conceived as the promotion of a new social order (Podgórecki, 1996).

On the promotional function of law, or the preeminent dependence on external factors, significant analyses can be found even by authors who are very different to each other[131], such as for example Niklas Luhmann, Norberto Bobbio and Lawrence M. Friedman. For his part, Henry Maine (1861), author of *Ancient Law*, claimed that juridical systems changed according to a defined temporal line, originating from the first Roman Code (*duodecim tabularum leges*) and leading to 19th century law. If Maine describes the evolution of law through the passage from "status" to "contract", Durkheim (1893), on the other hand, describes this sequence through the category of mechanical solidarity (which represents ancient society), and organic solidarity (characterising modern society). Weber also describes the development of law through the double criteria of

---

[129] According to Bentham, the legislature creates legal rules, which are qualified as commands. For Savigny, instead, the legislature records institutional practices socially widespread and sometimes already categorised by legal doctrine, then translating them into precepts.

[130] In Podgorecki's opinion, Law is represented as "*socjotechnika*" and it has the function to promote a new social order.

[131] Vilhelm Aubert and Norberto Bobbio, for example, believe that the law holds a promotional function that is essentially guaranteed by the application of positive sanctions.

"rationality/irrationality" and "formality/materialism" within the juridical system. Rational law is indeed universalistic and focalises on contract and not on status, while the irrational juridical system is particularistic (Weber, 1922). Philip Selznick proposed a theory which could be defined as "micro-evolution", which concentrates on how law develops in single organisations and/or in global societies (Selznick and Nonet, 1978). Instead, according to Friedman (1975), juridical evolutionism is based on considerations of a single type of progress and on a single perspective of development. Juridical systems in time become more or less legalistic, centralised, or litigious. Under the profile of the evolution of juridical norms, the legal system produces new norms and changes the form and the content of the older ones. Changes come about in two directions, from discretionary to objective and from objective to discretionary: the active elements pertaining to the legal system tend to modify themselves, reducing the area of discretion.

12. Resilience Law and Types of Change Described by Friedman

Before providing a first qualification of legal change, I am going to describe the theory on change in law according to Lawrence Friedman. In his view, the norms of "living law" tend towards objectivity and consider "living" the norms, which individuals use. Organs then apply that to real behaviour that can be contrasted or controversial. They establish themselves in two ways: 1) following social pressures, the legislator modifies norms replacing those empty terms, which determine discretion; and 2) through the splitting of a single generic norm into different precise and quantifiable parts. In this framework, no norm is completely stable (see e.g., Frank, 1930)[132]. According to Friedman's theories, change in law, in its most important forms, follows social changes and depends on them. However, not all changes that occur in a legal system regard the most important forms of change. Various modifications, indeed, are only minor, for example the addition of an article to an act. Therefore, some changes should not be necessarily qualified as a product of external social forces, but rather as a mere phenomenon within the legal system.

---

[132] In this sense, we could recall Jerome Frank, according to whom the results of a cause are never certain. Many things must be taken into account, for instance the personality of the Magistrate, the ability of the defence, the degree of trustworthiness of the witnesses and other parties, procedural evidence which could be taken into consideration due to procedural reasons.

Friedman distinguishes four types of juridical changes, with reference to the place of origin of the change and to the final place of impact: (1) changes which have origins outside the legal system, that is in society, but which concern only the system itself and end there; (2) changes which originate outside the legal system, but which pass through it towards a point of impact outside the law, upon society; (3) changes which arise from the legal system and exercise all their impact within the system itself; and (4) changes which originate within the legal system and which, proceeding through it, show their impact outside law, in society.

At this point, it would be opportune to ask ourselves how we should interpret the principle of 'resilience' in light of these divisions. The hypotheses of change that in my opinion most likely approach Resilience Law are the second and the fourth, as it is necessary to exclude the first and the third type of change, which are not consistent with the change that leads to Resilience Law. A different qualification of change in law, thus, emerges, considering these two types of changes identified by Friedman.

The first applicable hypothesis of change (corresponding to the second hypothesis described above) derives from outside the legal system and, passing through it, projects its effects towards society. Friedman distinguishes two types of change through law: "planning" and "disruption", where by 'disruption' he means those changes that can be seen with the destruction and dismantling of acknowledged juridical order, while 'planning' refers to the change that creates a new juridical order, which in the prospect of resilience could coincide with a "resilient juridical order". It is able to enhance reflexivity and polycentric governance, promoting the adaptability of the legal system itself.

The second applicable hypothesis of change (the fourth hypothesis described by Friedman) arises within the juridical system and from there has an impact on society. In relation to this kind of change, Friedman envisages a hypothesis according to which previous to any juridical change, some form of social change should be in the form of an act. If the contrary were to be affirmed, it would mean denying the fundamental presupposition of every legal theory as a social fact, giving excessive value to abstract norms and concepts.

A plausible customary nature of the principle of resilience could indicate that prior to legal change some form of social change, stimulated by "*consuetude*" (custom), must have taken place. As a matter of fact within this perspective, the vulnerabilities of people have determined conditions that make fundamental the use of the concept of resilience, which in practice has entered the common language, in order to understand and internalise the force necessary to oppose a critical condition (be it psychological, ecological, economic, ethical, social or otherwise).

In my opinion, though these aforementioned hypotheses are fascinating, they would probably be insufficient and inadequate to describe the change that actually took place in this area. In fact, I suppose instead that the change, which leads to Resilience Law, could have its origins both inside and outside the legal system and that, successively, it influences the social environment[133]. The principle of resilience in fact is a principle I could define as a 'meta-legal' norm, which encloses within itself a social, political, ethical and economic nature. It is capable of generating a change which arises simultaneously in the different systems and which will have an impact on society.

13. Change and Resilience According to Luhmannian Thinking

Niklas Luhmann, for his part, considers that a system evolves through the fulfilment of three functions: the production of possibilities of new types within a system, for the rest unchanged; the selection of the possibilities that can be used, excluding those that are unusable; and the stabilisation of the possibilities that can be used within the structure of the system. Luhmann also includes his special consideration on the evolution of the legal system, understood as a progressive differentiation of this system from other human communication systems, as well as a differentiation of the same system internally[134].

By the separation of the legal system from other systems, society equipped itself with a mechanism of selection of behaviour expectations that restricted the range of acceptable expectations, distinguishing those which were legitimate from those which weren't. Thus, human activity has gradually become more autonomous than other systems, becoming more rational and reliable (Luhmann, 1964).

---

[133] From a theoretical point of view, the change of law that takes place both outside and inside the legal system and that reverberates its effects on the social sphere is not connectable with the categories of change suggested by Friedman.

[134] About the sustainable dimension of the Luhmann perspectives, see: Wallis and Valentinov, 2016.

Focusing on research carried out by Luhmann, we could assume that change which gives origin to law on the subject of resilience could have its roots both in the ecological system and in socio-economic systems. In fact, the systems of social, ecological and economic laws connect to each other, establishing structural changes. These mutations come about through autopoietic operations thanks to which the same systems re-construct themselves, adding or eliminating elements by means of new functional requirements.

Given that 'resilience' is the other side of vulnerability, in this field different expectations emerge, in addition to various functional needs deriving from several areas (e.g., ethical, economic, ecological and social). The larger and general system of law adds all those elements that are able to realise the stability of incompatible expectations and get rid of all those elements that tend to oppose such stability[135] (Ruhl 1997, 933), as the latter tend to isolate themselves within their own structural complexity[136] (Morin, 1990) and incompatibility[137] (Fischman, 2019). In accordance with this view, Resilience Law might be interpreted as a "selection concerning further possibilities"[138]. Therefore, the resilience process would become a tool capable of responding to complexity and unpredictability.

14. Resilience Law as a Sociocultural Change?

In accordance with another theoretical dimension, we could qualify "Resilience Law" as a sociocultural change. The term "culture" can be defined in different ways: for instance, we could define it as the way of life for people or as the tool by which the members of a society share a common ancestry. The great weakness of the ecological-evolutionary theory has been represented by the lack of systematic development of the interrelationships

---

[135] Considering the complex nature of the legal system, Ruhl (1997) notes that legal systems can be defined in terms of their structure and functions, and therefore such systems exhibit features of both stability and change that operate at multiple scales.
[136] According to Edgar Morin, the "complex method" is intended to understand the differences and fragmentations not as exceptions to the supposed rules, but as natural and autonomous forms of expression linked to a reality that is born in itself differentiated.
[137] In accordance with Fishman, letting go of stability releases us from untenable expectations of the steady maintenance of some natural order.
[138] An expression frequently used by Luhmann.

between the material infrastructure, the social structure and the cultural superstructure of societies (Elwell, 2013).

Gerhard Lenski, for instance, explains that one of the basic principles of the modern evolutionary theory is that the evolutionary process itself evolves (Lenski, 2005). Sociocultural evolution depends upon symbol-based cultural information, which can be transmitted across cultures.

In Lenski's view, societies are sociocultural systems with component parts fitting loosely together to form a coherent whole (Lenski, 2005). They are loose systems, very imperfect, where not all parts benefit equally in the distribution of resources. Lenski also recognises a global system as the totality of human societies and their interrelationships. In his opinion, sociocultural change is often rooted in changes in the environment caused by spontaneous natural forces (such as ice ages) or human activities (pollution, resource depletion, cultural diffusion). Moreover, Max Weber's rationalisation theory relates very well to each component of the sociocultural system.

The link between law, resilience and sociocultural evolution is more evident especially if we consider the customary nature of law in the field of resilience.

In this regard, Jeremy Bentham and John Austin believed that customary law was a contradiction in terms (Bentham, 2010). For Hart and other theorists, instead, the internalisation of a rule of recognition is a necessary and sufficient condition for the existence of law (Hart, 1961). Frederick Schauer, on the other hand, maintains that the custom/practice, linked to the status of law, must be a normative custom and not only a description of a non-normative empirical regularity. Internalised normative custom is law and, in large part, law is internalised custom (Schauer, 2013, 523).

Indeed, the resilience principle can be considered as an emerging principle of customary law (Sands, 2003; Kiss and Shelton, 1994; Voigt, 2009; Hunter et al., 2001). It, in fact, finds its binding reason in "custom", identified in its social, ethical, political, economic and legal dimensions.

"Customary rule" develops spontaneously and proposes itself as a model of expectation of behaviour, characterised by prolonged use, which may be accepted within public opinion, by virtue of which this must not be transgressed. This norm is strengthened by use of authoritarian terms, such as in this case the words "resilient" and "resilience".

From another point of view, Resilience Law could be seen as a sociocultural change that finds an epistemic and ontological matrix in transnational law. In fact, if we wanted to attribute a space-time location to the relationship between resilience and law, we could recognise in transnationality an adequate theoretical categorisation. Transnational law, in effect, allows for space beyond some of the predefined theoretical pillars, which oscillate between "within" and "outside" the western space boundaries, "before" and "after" globalisation (Zumbansen, 2015, 5), and "behind" and "beneath" traditional theoretical canons (Zumbansen, 2014).

Philip Jessup stated that transnational law intended to include all law regulating actions or events that transcend national frontiers (Jessup, 1956, 2; Zumbansen, 2008, 738). Twining speaks about "sustainable critique" (Twining, 2000, 10-13; De Sousa Santos, 1987, 279-280; Zumbansen 2015), with reference to a conceptual semantic apparatus through which a cross-cultural, transnational dialogue could be realistic. Transnational law would therefore describe new areas of legal, economic, political and cultural contestation (Zumbansen, 2015, 9).

Philip Allott, for his part, refers to an "international unsociety" of so-called sovereign States, and in this regard, the "ghost of pre-democratic, pre-socialized society would come to haunt the whole world, distorting and deranging all human socializing" (Allott 1992, 244; Allott, 1990).

Resilience is undoubtedly a theoretical question, in the sense used by Twining of a "theory in action", which concerns a broader vision that crosses spatial and temporal boundaries and knows how to look from above according to common cosmopolitan criteria.

15. The Change of Law through Transfer, Spread, Transmission, Imitation, Transplant, Convergence, Circulation, Borrowing, Globalisation, Diffusion or "Interaction"?

Until the early 1970s, the law was regarded as the product of socioeconomic and cultural situations in a given place (Watson, 1974; Watson, 1976; Watson, 1977; Watson, 1984; Watson, 1985). Subsequently, the idea of the social system and the legal structure as parallel systems was widely debated (Wise, 1990; Schauer, 2000; Rodière, 1978; Tamanaha, 2001; Gaudemet 1976; Rouland, 1988).

The evolution of law can be explained also through the circulation of knowledge, or rather through criteria such as transfer, imitation, transplant, convergence, borrowing, globalisation, and the diffusion of law and policies.

According to Roscoe Pound, the history of a system of law is a history of "borrowings" of legal materials from other legal systems, that is to say, an assimilation process concerning matters from outside the law (Pound, 1938). Alan Watson spoke about the "transfer" of a rule from one legal system to another, as well as from one person to another (Watson, 1974). According to him, borrowing is the best source of legal change (Watson, 1996, 335).

Tseming Yang and Robert Percival, instead, consider the spread of legal models to be a convergence more than a transplant (Yang 2009, 615). This convergence is mainly represented by the global propagation of approaches and ideas (Busch and Jorgens, 2012).

Similarly, Edward M. Wise underlines the concept of "circulation" rather than that of a "transplant" or "borrowing" (Wise, 1990).

The literature on the "diffusion of law" does not belong to a single research tradition. In this sense, Twining recalls the writings of Gabriel Tarde, Sir Henry Maine and Max Weber, stating that: "diffusionism represented a reaction against the prevailing nineteenth century view that there were natural laws of evolution governing human progress" (Twining, 2009, 273). Conversely, Trisha Greenhalgh suggests that much of the social science literature on diffusion of innovations belongs to a single research tradition, although it is located in different branches of sociology (Greenhalgh, 2004).

In the field of resilience, I think we should speak about "interaction", more than borrowing, spread, transmission, transplant, diffusion, transfer, imitation, convergence, globalisation[139] or circulation[140]. With regard to globalisation, the globalisation of the cultural model on resilience is not developed only by the imitation of legislations, policies and best practices

---

[139] The globalisation of the cultural model on resilience is not developed only by the imitation of legislations, policies and best practices coming from other countries, but also by the implementation of multi-level standards of a moral, political, legal, ethical or economic nature.

[140] In the French language, we find these terms: 'diffusion', 'emprunt', 'imitation', 'propagation', 'réception', 'transfert', 'migration', and 'transposition'.

coming from other countries, but also by the implementation of multi-level standards of a moral, political, legal, ethical or economic nature (See e.g.: Morand Deviller and Bénichot, 2010; Shapiro, 1993, 51; Tews, 2011, 227-252).

In this matter, indeed, the interactions among different sectors and skills forged the change that has contributed to the creation of a substantial "resilience science". These interactions not only include the spheres of law or politics, but also economics, ethics and social sciences.

16. Some Considerations about Resilience Framework and Law

The law on the subject of sustainability has the function of solving potential conflicts among different typologies of norms. Although there are multiple definitions of sustainability, "sustainability law" has developed to the point of generating important theoretical transformations. In this regard, I have also identified the category of emergency sustainability, which is associated with emergencies arising from critical situations, including those linked to disaster management. It is intended as a new possibility with which to interpret sustainability, something nowadays that is characterised by increasingly catastrophic scenarios. In line with this view and within the most diverse disciplinary categories, the concept of resilience clearly emerges.

There is no single theoretical qualification about the concept of resilience. However, there are several conceptual apparatuses that seem to move in the direction of resilience. In common, these different ways of understanding resilience have an epistemic background of "complexity", because in the face of globalisation, resilience would appear a useful tool to create an "order", capable of giving balance and harmony in every field in which it expresses itself.

Law has underlined a concept that by this time seems to have taken the place of the same notion of 'sustainability'. In effect, a growing interest in resilience as a feature of communities and cultural groups is emerging. In my opinion, resilience is the postmodern metaphor of ethical management of change, which is particularly important for the climate change and disasters issues and other human and social crises.

As Fischman claims, managing resilience as a law objective will promise less than sustainability, but deliver more of what it promises (Fischman, 2019).

The local dimension where the process of resilience develops, also through the establishment of local networks, is combined with a transnational theoretical dimension, which adequately welcomes the theoretical-practical relationship between law and resilience frameworks.

This work has tried to better understand the emergence of the concept of resilience in law, through theoretical categories such as the evolution of law, which can be explained by different theories. From this analysis, it emerges that Resilience Law has its origins both inside and outside the legal system and it influences the social and ethical sphere. The resilience principle can in fact be considered as a meta-legal norm. The resilience paradigm is also a tool capable of responding to complexity and unpredictability. In fact, it is the result of "interaction" among different scientific fields. However, it is also a sociocultural change, both from the point of view of the "customary rule" and from that of transnational law.

At this point, I will try to outline a new theoretical scenario that fits within the emergency sustainability vision, and that considers the theoretical framework on equity, in relation to resilience, ethics and law.

17. The Link Between Resilience and Sustainability

We have already shown how the concepts of resilience and sustainability are very similar to each other, so much so that we could even hypothesise that the first concept is the theoretical heir of the second. Even if this were not the case, it would be possible to assert that the notion of resilience certainly constitutes a fundamental theoretical aspect of guaranteeing sustainability.

The legal theories on resilience, moreover, fit perfectly into my theoretical proposal of "emergency sustainability", because a theoretical framework on resilience, in whatever sense we want to consider this term, is a fundamental pillar to safeguard a minimum threshold of sustainability in the presence of a crisis or an emergency situation. Resilience law is a relatively new theoretical apparatus, which however is limited in operational terms. Therefore, in order for this legal framework to represent a valid theoretical matrix within the framework of "emergency sustainability", this law must be an "equitable law". In other words, resilience can work well through law, only if it uses a particular ethical criterion, that is to say the "equity" criterion. It concerns both the present and future natural resources of the planet (or, if we wish, of the Universe), as well as present and future human and non-human (vegetable or animal) generations. From this point of view, I could say that resilience maintains a "futuristic" vision, which is guaranteed precisely by equity.

In effect, resilience intervenes in crisis situations that are often determined by a discrepancy among different balances, or rather by phenomena of "disequity" and therefore by regimes in which equity is marginalised. The degree of emergency may arise or increase from this "*diminutio*".

In this sense, for instance, is the expression "emergency law"[141] which - after the advent of Covid-19 - has been spreading in the cultural landscape, perhaps to be understood as an "exception law" or rather as an "exception of law"? Sometimes, in fact, emergencies tend to overturn the very foundations of law, denying fundamental freedoms and rights in the name of collective security. The law governing a catastrophic emergency is only an instrument to be considered in the context of "resilience law", provided that this is limited to regulate a state of exception, capable of moderating and balancing the various rights involved in the scenario of emergency considered. If this balance is not guaranteed, then "emergency law" cannot be represented as a tool capable of promoting "resilience".

In the next paragraphs, therefore, I will be arguing about the relationship between equity and law, sketching a brief history of the concept of equity within legal sources. Subsequently, in the aforementioned futuristic perspective, I will dedicate a paragraph to the rights and duties regarding future generations, which in my opinion do not constitute an anthropocentric vision of sustainability, but rather lead to the reflection that too many imbalances cause injury to human dignity, as well as to dignity of every form existing in nature. Some of these injuries now seem incurable.

18. Equitable Resilience

The next paragraphs will consider equity as a theoretical premise of the resilience framework and therefore as a valid link between resilience and sustainability, presenting a resilient equity, able to pursue sustainable resilience

---

[141] For example, I proposed the expression "*Emergency Sustainability*", as well as the acronym "*KatastLaw*", referring with this last term to the law of man-made or natural catastrophes.

objectives in ethical scenarios increasingly characterised by crisis. Finally, through some conclusions, the theoretical framework analysed will certainly appear more homogeneous from an epistemic point of view.

19. Equity and Law

For the ancient Romans, equity and justice are two different theoretical categories. An *iustum* behaviour, in fact, could be considered *aequum*, as well as *iniquum*; similarly, an *iniustum* behaviour could still be considered *aequum* (Maruotti, 2012).

Cicero, for example, believed that equity should permeate the *ius*, thus being within the law, not just outside it. Therefore, the law was equitable when it met real social needs. The *ius civile* was therefore *aequabilis* because it retained in itself the ability to reduce to equality, in the sense of "*ius suum cuique tribuere*". Until the classical age, the *aequum/iniquum* categories supported the adherence of the norms to the social conscience.

The glossers, instead, identified in God the sources of equity. Starting from a few moral and ethical standards of religious matrix, they reworked the comprehensive system of rules of Roman law. For them, equity was an instrument of mediation between Justinian law and particular rights, as well as between the *Lex Mundana* and the *Lex Ecclesiastica*. Therefore, equity represented the source of natural justice that was intrinsic to human relationships by divine will and was adapted to feelings of "*humanitas*".

In the canonical *aequitas*, equity takes on the connotations of divine order and justice: "*nihil aliud est aequitas quam Deus*". The values of *charitas*, *misericordia*, *humanitas* and *benignitas* therefore followed, as opposed to *iustitia*, understood as *rigor iuris*.

Even in common law, equity has played an important role. The jurisdiction of equity concerned precisely that sector of Anglo-Saxon law developed from the fourteenth century A.D. and characterised by the prevalence of the Roman-canonic *aequitas*. The name "equity" derived from the Chancellor *aequitas*. The crisis of the English courts began when King Henry III interrupted the writs system by a formal act in 1258. Subjects turned to the king with a plea to obtain justice. The petitions were presented to the Bishop Chancellor (Chancellor), since as a spiritual guide of the king he granted the remedy that the courts were no longer able to grant. The trust, for example, is an institution that comes from an equity regime.

Currently, different interpretations of this concept exist. For instance, the judge Weeramantry[142] quotes Aristotle's *Nicomachean Ethics*. In this regard, equity assumes the role of "mitigation of the application of rigid rules". He believes that, in the distribution of natural resources, equity is playing an increasingly central role. In this perspective, the principle of equity can be used in the sense of applying distributive justice and the redistribution of wealth. In another decision, indeed, the International Court of Justice ruled that equity as a legal concept was "a direct emanation of the idea of justice"[143].

According to the IPCC (2014), "equity" is an integral dimension of sustainable development and it is supposed by three criteria: (1) a "moral" justification that draws upon ethical principles; (2) a "legal" justification that appeals to existing treaty commitments and soft law agreements in order to cooperate in accordance with equity principles; and (3) an "effectiveness" justification by virtue of which a fair arrangement is more likely to be agreed internationally and successfully implemented domestically. However, the question of the role that equity should play in the establishment of global climate policy and burden sharing in particular is certainly controversial. Nevertheless, the IPCC (2014) identifies some principles as corollaries of equity. These principles are: "responsibility", "capacity", "right to development" and "equality".

Through the concept of sustainable development, an equity framework has evolved particularly in favour of future generations. Therefore, below, I will explain the main theories that have been developing about the rights and duties associated with these generations.

20. Equity Applied to Climate Law and Policy

On the subject of equitable emissions, several principles are relevant. To the principle of the 'guaranteed minimum', for which a minimum level of resources (i.e., a *minimum* of economic development) must be ensured, is added a norm that tells us about who has the burden of redistributing and sanctioning inequalities, that is to say the "principle of the greater capacity", under which those who have greater portions of a given common good must contribute more to the redistribution of that good. In the field of climate

---

142 International Court of Justice. 1997. Gabcíkovo-Nagymaros Project (Hungary/Slovakia), par. 118 (d).

143 International Court of Justice. 1982. Continental Shelf (Tunisia/Libyan Arab Jamahiriya), par. 71.

change this would mean that those with greater capacity must contribute more to total emission reductions.

The "principle of equal percentages", then, requires each State to limit its own emissions, equal in percentage to all States. However, asking for the same percentage of reduction to a developing country and an industrialised nation would mean not guaranteeing the first one some right to development.

Even the "principle of equal burdens", of which Traxler is a promoter, aims to make equal the opportunities lost by the different States (Traxler, 2002), through the reduction of emissions (Moellendorf, 2009). However, this principle does not consider the level of wealth and development of a country and ignores the distinction between luxury goods and livelihoods. The more developed countries would lose the opportunity to continue to extend their luxury consumption, while developing countries would no longer have the opportunity to ensure subsistence.

The "principle of equal sacrifice", on the other hand, means that no reductions can be made in countries where endemic poverty exists. Reduction allowances are therefore divided among other nations, so that the resulting costs are the same for all countries.

Last but not least, the principle of "equal per capita parts" is the principle by which each State should reduce its own emissions to the level that would be obtained by multiplying the population at a given time for the average per capita emissions granted, relative to the global reduction needed to achieve a certain degree of concentration. This principle adheres to the principle of "common but differentiated responsibilities", as it requires a substantial reduction in industrialised countries, which have a higher per capita emissions rate, while it allows developing countries, with low per capita emissions, to increase their consumption.

Nevertheless, it is certainly not free of criticism. Indeed, it would be sufficient to set higher levels of global reduction to ensure that even developing countries are required to make onerous sacrifices (Baer, Kartha, Athanasiou and Kemp-Benedict, 2009, 6). Even for developed countries, this principle can be very demanding. Generally, we could say that it does not take into account the different levels of development of the various countries. A matter that conflicts with the validity of an approach of "equal per capita parts" was also dealt with by Amartya Sen, who believes it is wrong for theories of distributive justice to focus on "resources" (as in Dworkin) or what Rawls calls 'primary goods'. On this topic, Caney notes:

"it is therefore implausible to focus on distributing one particular resource equally if doing so will leave people unequal in their ability to pursue various goals" (Caney, 2009, 2).

A variant of the model on per capita equitable emissions is also found in the proposal known as "contraction and convergence" developed by the Global Commons Institute and advanced in 1996 at the Second Climate Conference (COP2) held in Geneva. The proposal focuses on an equitable model of distribution of responsibilities and allocation of emission permits that allows industrialised countries to progressively reduce their emissions and developing countries to intensify them gradually until, after a transition period, each State gets the same emission rights. More specifically, the model suggests a dual strategy, capable of causing a contraction of greenhouse gas emissions from industrialised countries at first, and subsequently a convergence towards equal levels of per capita emissions for all countries. The date for convergence is set for 2045, the year of the United Nations centenary. The goal of the contraction is to associate the various responsibilities with the historical contribution to global warming. Convergence, however, aims to distribute future CO2 emission rights, so that each country has the same per capita level (by 2045). This model, which also promotes technology transfer, financial flows and carbon trading, has evolved over time, resulting in new theoretical models such as *Cap and Share* and the *Greenhouse Development Rights* framework.

The right to development or even the right to greenhouse gas emissions requires that each State receives a right of emission in the light of its own responsibility (Caney, 2005). The notion of "right to development" makes sense to the extent that a right to an emission quota can be an appropriate tool to meet its own core needs. There is no right to meet one's own basic needs through the production of greenhouse gases. This principle would also distribute costs independently of the benefits and disadvantages (Miller, 2008). The model of contraction and convergence was adopted by the Indian Government and later in 1997 by the African Group of Negotiators on Climate Change.

Posner and Weisbach, for their part, believe that if carbon dioxide emissions were combined with the impact of deforestation and urbanisation, from 1950 to today, China, Russia and Indonesia would be at the top for historical contribution to global warming (after the United States). If we calculate the per capita emissions in the same period, we would find instead at the top countries such as Belize, Guyana and Luxembourg, characterised by inadequate production facilities (Posner and Weisbach, 2010). Therefore, if we apply the principle of historical responsibility, we should stop the economic development of countries such as China and India, asking them to reduce their emissions to zero. Moreover, for these authors, the principle of historical responsibility is unreasonable: it cannot be understood in fact why present generations should pay for the actions taken by their ancestors.

Despite this, it is true that these generations enjoy the benefits of the unjust actions of their ancestors, although due to the effects of pollution, they have also inherited several damages, not just benefits.

The "White Paper on the Ethical Dimensions of Climate Change", produced by Donald Brown *et alias* (2013) in his "Program on the ethical dimensions of climate change", published by the University of Pennsylvania, begins its discussion by describing some sources such as the Rio Declaration (1992), in particular Principles 2 and 16, and the Framework Convention on Climate Change (Article 3). The "White Paper" states that developing countries have various responsibilities, including making every effort to support sustainable development practices (Brown, 2013).

One responsibility is described as the duty to participate in a global, fair system of greenhouse gas emissions. Even if developed countries were to cease their emissions, global warming would still represent a serious problem. The "White Paper" presents several ethical approaches, the most relevant of which is inherent in the equitable allocations of per capita emissions. It is based on the idea that all human beings should be aiming at equitable sharing of the common good "atmosphere". The approach based on equity and applied to greenhouse gas emissions also requires that all individuals have the right to emit an equitable amount of carbon dioxide.

Personally, I think the theme of responsibility for climate change is somewhat delicate and reflects above all the economic interests of the various countries. International political documents in fact are the mirror of these interests, and sometimes these seem to take a few steps forward in order to tackle climate change issues, but other times instead they silently back down.

21. Equitable Responsibility for Future Generations

Equitable responsibility suggests a cooperative model and, hence, an intergenerational and intra-generational equity. If we were to forget that sustainability must ensure fairness in the way in which we consider present and future generations, we would run the risk of devaluing the content of the sustainable responsibility. The intergenerational nature of sustainable responsibility is easier to understand when examined in a comparison with certain relevant virtues and with the integrity principle.

The principle of intergenerational equity is understood as a programmatic provision that requires Member States to keep in consideration the needs not only of the present generation, but also of future generations, stressing the importance of a rational use of natural resources. For instance, Article 2 of the Convention on Biological Diversity (Nairobi, 1992) shows the intergenerational equity in the definition of sustainable use. Let us also mention the Rio Declaration that associates intergenerational equity with the right of development, stating that this right must be satisfied "so as to equitably meet developmental and environmental needs of present and future generations". This Declaration has been joined to a policy document, Agenda 21, which outlines the process aimed at sustainable development by proposing targets placed in a perspective of equity. The principle of intra-generational equity, instead, allows each State to respond in the implementation of its policies to the needs of its own country and of other countries, recalling the dutifulness of all States to cooperate so as to achieve a common goal. Intra-generational equity refers to the duty of cooperation expressed in Principle 5 of the Rio Declaration, according to which all States and people should cooperate in the essential task of eradicating poverty, described as a prerequisite for sustainable development, in order to decrease disparities in standards of living and satisfy the needs of most people in the world.

22. Equity and Resilience for Future Generations: Between Rights and Duties

This section refers to the elaboration of a set of theories on rights and duties related to future generations. From this point of view, intergenerational responsibility may be also established within a legal framework, especially intended as social technical[144]. Future generations, in fact, are protected, providing that legal systems put in place appropriate instruments, regardless of the values to be preserved.

Now, we can think about the supposed impossibility of recognising rights or other subjective legal situations for those who do not exist yet. It could be argued that future generations hold legal capacity, although they

[144] Kelsen declares the law could substantially be a social technique.

lack the capacity to act. This gap can however be overcome thanks to the institution of representation. The same World Commission on Environment and Development recommended the appointment of an advocate for future generations. At the Conference of Rio de Janeiro, the Government of Malta suggested the nomination of a "guardian", without decision-making powers, with the task of representing the interests of future generations in various international headquarters. The Maltese proposal, however, was only mentioned in Agenda XXI. The idea of an "ombudsman" for future generations was proposed even at Rio+20 in June 2012, though it was not reproduced in the final declaration. Furthermore, it was also recommended by Kornélia (Kornélia, 2012). Ward, instead, was influenced by the Hungarian Parliamentary Commissioner for Future Generations (Ward, 2009). Economic and ecological interdependence has transformed the international society into a "domestic society where nation-states just like individual members are accountable to each other and to future generations as custodians of the world environment" (Baslar, 1998).

Other scholars speak about "future conditional rights", which require the existence of interests that are independent from abstract qualifications (Gosseries, 2008). In the absence of specific people, the legal system can in fact protect the interests of the same and therefore function in subjective legal situations. Despite the lack of future individuals, the obligation of those who undertake the actions in question (in this case, the present generation) still exists. To "representation" and "future conditional rights", qualified as instruments to support the ownership of rights towards the future generations, we can, without any doubt, approach the "fiction" (or the *fictio* of the roman law), beyond the institution of the "trust".

On the concept of a "trust" applied to future generations, the theoretical development proposed by Brown Weiss certainly stands out. It is based on the concept of "planetary trust", built on the principles of common law that support precisely this *trust*. The function of this institution is to protect the welfare of future generations and intergenerational equity; the fiduciary obligation towards future generations may be classified among general international standards, as the production of an obligation "*erga omnes*".

The idea that as members of present generation we hold the earth in *trust* for future generations, in fact, is known in international law. The concept of *trust* recognises its own historical origin in the institute of Roman law called "*fiducia*" (*fiducia cum amico* and *fiducia cum creditore*). The setting of the theoretical framework of Edith Brown Weiss particularly interests the study of the rights and duties under an intergenerational perspective (Brown Weiss 1993, 333). Brown Weiss defines three principles of intergenerational equity based on (1) options, (2) quality and (3) access for the next generation (Brown Weiss, 1992). "Access" refers to the need for current generations to provide equitable admission to their legacy. The intergenerational duties include 1. the obligation to pass on the Earth to the next generation in the same state received from the previous generation; and 2. the obligation to repair any damage resulted from a failure of the previous generations in relation to that obligation. From this point of view, each generation should: a) preserve the natural and cultural diversity of the Earth, b) monitor and improve environmental quality, c) ensure every individual fair access of natural resources inherited from previous generations, and d) maintain this equitable access for future generations. Rights are associated with obligations and therefore more specifically the right of future generations to receive the Earth in a condition no worse than that in which it has been received by the present generation; the right to benefit from a non-altered natural and cultural diversity; the right to equitable access to natural resources; and the right to environmental quality.

Laura Westra, for instance, emphasises the combination of the concept of integrity and that of common good, in view of a protection for the benefit of future generations (Westra, 1998). According to her, eco-crime concerning present and future generations essentially focuses on "institutionalised" violence against the environment, which is synonymous with human rights violations. Institutionalised exchange of greenhouse gases emissions quotas, in fact, amount to a compromise between the law and the ability to pollute and thus deface the environment, altering the climate (Westra, 2006).

Furthermore, in line with Donald A. Brown and Prue Taylor, there is "little hope that the international community will be able to prevent dangerous climate change and as a result of that hundreds of millions of the poorest people in the world and future generations will suffer the harshest consequences" (Brown and Taylor, 2014).

Keeping present the language of the Universal Declaration of Human Rights (1948), Weiss concludes that: "the reference to all members of the human family has a temporal dimension which brings all generations within its scope. The reference to the equal and inalienable rights, affirms the basic equality of such generations in the human family" (Brown Weiss, 1992) According to Sands, instead, future generations' rights could enhance "the legal standing of members of the present generation to bring claims in cases relying upon substantive rules of environmental Treaties where doubt exists as to whether a particular creates treaty rights and obligations enforceable by individuals" (Sands, 1995, 200).

23. Intergenerational Equity and Law Cases

Intergenerational equity is clearly visible in some legal cases, promoted by children and young people in favour of future generations. Although often these cases do not lead to a real protection of the younger and future generations, they are singular for their highly ethical nature. Even if guided by adults, these children know very well that their rights are violated in the face of increasingly selfish powers, which are represented by our governments, which fail to do the common good, in order to do instead what is most convenient for their lobbies.

First, I recall the "*Minors Oposa vs. Secretary of the Department of Environmental and Natural Resources*" case (1993), where the Supreme Court of the Philippines enshrined the principle according to which future generations are entitled to take legal action to enforce rights with environmental protection. The complainants were forty Filipino minors (accompanied by thirty-six parents) and a non-governmental organisation from the Philippines (Philippine Ecological Network, Inc.); they sued an organ of the National Government, the Secretary of the Department of Environment and Natural Resources of the Philippines. The applicants claimed the right to prevent the damage to the rainforests of the Philippines and to stop the relentless haemorrhage of vital life support systems of the country and the continuing violence against Mother Earth. More precisely, they asked the judge to order the defendant to cancel all licenses of national exploitation of wood and not to release or renew any further licenses. In only twenty-five years, in fact, the extent of the territory occupied by rainforests had been reduced from 53% to 2.8% and, given the current rate of deforestation, it was reasonable to believe that the Philippines would have lost in a few years every area of its rainforest. For the plaintiff, therefore, the refusal of the Secretary of the Department of Environment and Natural Resources of the Philippines to cancel the licenses constituted a clear violation of the right to enjoy a healthy and balanced environment. On the contrary, the defendant believed that the plaintiffs were without legal standing and noted that the case had a political nature and not a legal one. According to Section 16 of the Philippine Constitution of 1987: "the State shall protect and advance the right of the people to a balanced and healthful ecology in tune with the rhythm and harmony of nature". The Court underlined section 2 of Presidential Decree 6 June 1977, n. 1151, which confers upon every generation of Filipinos the role of trustee and custodian of the environment for future generations. For the Court, moreover, the right to a balanced ecology also holds a higher value than the rules of constitutional status, since that right is linked to self-preservation as much as self-reproduction of the human race. The judge ultimately accepted the principle that minors could represent not only themselves and those belonging to their own generation, but future generations too.

The lawsuit submitted to the Supreme Court of Sri Lanka, *Deshan Harinda (a minor) et al. vs. Ceylon Electricity Board et al.* (also known as the "Kotte Kids" case, 1998) is also significant in this theoretical framework, as a group of children promoted a legal proceeding in which they stated that the noise from a power plant exceeded the allowable noise level, causing hearing loss amongst other things. Although the Constitution of Sri Lanka did not expressly impose the right to life, it was argued that all other constitutionally enshrined rights necessarily presupposed the existence of this right.

Even in the "Future Generations v. Ministry of the Environment et al." case (2018), 25 plaintiffs, being between 7 and 26 years old, brought legal action against several Colombian agencies and municipalities, in order to enforce their rights to a healthy environment and life. According to the plaintiffs, climate change, as well as the numerous administrative omissions aimed at reducing deforestation, would threaten their own basic rights. On April 5, 2018, the Supreme Court recognised the Colombian Amazon as a subject of rights needing protection and conservation.

On September 23, 2019, 16 children filed a petition before the United Nations Committee on the Rights of the Child (UNCRC) against the governments of Argentina, France, Turkey, Germany and Brazil, stating that their rights under the UNCRC had been violated, due to the omissions of governments themselves, with respect to cuts in greenhouse gas emissions, and the implementation of policies aimed at encouraging, rather than discouraging, the behaviour of the major carbon emitters, such as China, the United States, India and the European Union. Children, including the famous Greta Thunberg, lamented how these powers had not understood that climate change is equivalent to the crisis of their respective rights. Despite Brazil, France and Germany replying that this petition was not admissible, conversely the children stated the full competence of the consulted body, arguing that they are and will be forever harmed by the actions of those governments ("Sacchi et al. v. Argentina et al.", 2019).

In the "Juliana v. United States" case (2020), 21 children filed a complaint against the United States federal government, as they believed it had infringed their own rights, due to high concentrations of carbon dioxide, demanding that the government implemented a plan able to delete (bit-by-bit) dangerous emissions. The Court of Appeal (Ninth Circuit) dismissed this case, although the judges were aware of the apocalyptic scope of climate change (the sentence speaks of the "point of no return"), as well as the responsibilities of the USA, through their emissions and use of fossil fuels. Moreover, this "dismission" was decided despite the Court itself having verified the causal link between injuries suffered and emissions. Therefore, the Court declared its inability to judge on that subject matter, as according to judges the competence would lie with the legislator.

24. Equity and the Resilience of Non-Human Resources of the Universe: Towards a "Resilient Equity" in the Direction of the Emergency Sustainability Vision

Often, equity has involved aspects of intergenerational justice, leaving out interspecies justice, concerning the well-being of non-human (vegetable and animal) species, both present and future.

This last well-being, however, must not be considered in a utilitarian and instrumental way with respect to human well-being. The two well-beings are in fact parallel to each other and head towards a framework of epistemic health (Grasso, 2019).

The ethics underlying emergency sustainability guarantees an equitable procedure that allows resilience mechanisms to be put in place, which in turn involve both present and future generations, as well as the resources of the universe.

If equity for future generations responds to the need to ensure that these generations can enjoy a healthy land, equally, then equity for plant and animal resources responds to the need to guarantee the same resources and the possibility of continuing to live and reproduce. In this sense, therefore, equity ensures the pursuit of a harmonious balance that constitutes the theoretical presupposition in which the concepts of "resilience", "sustainability" and "law" can peacefully coexist, thus allowing the balanced survival[145] of the entire planet, and thus of the whole Universe. From this point of view, the concept of survival would seem to summarise the soul of this balance.

In light of the above, if equity represents the theoretical assumption of resilience, which in turn fully falls within my sustainability vision (as emergency sustainability), it follows that I could easily argue in favour of a "Resilient Equity", which pursues the aims of "Critical Justice", that is to say the form of justice that I have hypothesised for the emergency sustainability and that I have already mentioned in the first section.

25. Resilience Law, Vulnerability, Resistance and Rights: Which Theoretical Relationship?

"Resilience Law" can be considered as a model of social and juridical regulation that takes into account legal norms, as well as spontaneously consolidated social norms outside programmed forms of social control. The crisis of the State is a prerequisite within this scenario and, as Alberto Febbrajo recalls, when it comes to the crisis of the state it is easy to refer the term both to the legal models developed in the operational context and to the realities that should correspond to these models. Both aspects end up appearing as two sides of the same coin (Febbrajo, 2013, 26).

National and supranational crises, in fact, strengthen the "right to react" to paralysis, that is an "anti-nihilistic" right, which is opposed to omissions, and the right that shelters human and collective vulnerabilities, and that seeks to resist shock. Society is required to have a new way of dealing with critical situations. To do this, a matrix of law that increasingly follows social needs and vulnerabilities is needed, and therefore one which values the rights of the most vulnerable, who are often compromised in the face of confused and inhomogeneous global scenarios which inevitably generate inequality.

[145] As said by Hart, if we consider survival as a law's ultimate aim, we could understand the possible connection between law and morality. For Hart, law and morality cooperate toward the guarantee of human survival. Furthermore, the present generation is related from a legal point of view with future generations whenever human action is determined to change the conditions necessary for human survival. Some of the effects of human actions, in fact, are able to put at risk the very survival of humankind due to their grave effect on the environment.

The attention of law to vulnerability can refer to subjects who are holders of rights, so to speak "compressed", but at the same time it can also refer to a quality of modern law, which appears increasingly vulnerable. Its vulnerability can be seen in uncertainties, contradictions, legal gaps, fragmentation, excessive regulation and interpretative confusion.

In the "Elogio della mitezza" ("In Praise of Meekness"), Norberto Bobbio saw meekness as an important moral virtue (Bobbio, 2014). Similarly, Manuel Atienza sees in meekness that ductility or ability to adapt to the multiplicity of concrete cases (Atienza, 2010), with respect to which the hardness of the law is deaf, but to which the argumentative and interpretative practice of the law must give reasonable answers, which will be more effective to the extent that vulnerability is conceived as an instrumental quality of the law itself (Ciaramelli, 2018, 180).

Resilience Law, in some ways, could be interpreted as a type of justice, which tends to individual and collective perseverance with respect to the challenges that this new century places before us.

Resilience Law is in any case a law, in a metaphysical sense, which although it maintains its vulnerable character, at the same time manifests the desire to deal with situations characterised by a weakening of rights caused by individual and social vulnerabilities of a different nature.

I do not think that "meekness" can be considered a connotation of this law. Rather, I believe that the characters of "sensitivity" or "softness" must be considered within this framework. Resilience Law in fact should be sensitive, as it considers social issues that affect "vulnera", or wounds, which can have different causes. But it must also be "flexible", because it must easily be able to cope with the various contradictions, bureaucratisations and legal-political omissions, as well as with the difficulties that stand in the way of the "cure" of several vulnerabilities.

This process should be guided by legal practitioners, that is to say jurists, who should take on the task of raising awareness of the law, making it more adaptive to the most varied social contexts.

Resilience Law should consider the possibility of "resisting". After all, resilience really means "resistance". Resisting to what? For example, to injustices or inequities that widen the wounds causing the vulnerability that is being considered.

The "Right of Resistance" is the right to resist an unjust order. Disobedience is lawful if the law is unjust (that is, it does not correspond to the principles of justice), illegitimate (since it is issued by someone who does not have the power) or invalid (that is to say, contrary to the current Constitutions). In this sense, I recall the "theory of the legitimacy of resistance to the tyrant", formulated by John Locke, or Thoreau's civil disobedience, which requires that human conscience takes precedence over the law, and which criticises social institutions and policies, with particular regard to slavery and war (Thoreau, 1849).

According to the scholar Passerin d'Entreves, there are different types of disobedient behaviour against the law: civil disobedience, passive resistance and active resistance. Resistance can be omissive or commissive, individual or collective, clandestine or public, peaceful or violent, passive (because it accepts the sentence) or active (evades the sentence) (Passerin d'Entrèves, 2018).

Ultimately, this form of justice (Resilience Law) affects both the category represented by the relationship between "rights and vulnerability", as well as the relationship between "rights and resistance". It is a form of justice that should in my opinion be concerned with the numerous inequalities that climatic, political and social challenges present us with and will continue to present us with in the near future.

26. Conclusions

This work began with the study of sustainability theories applied to law and – by examining the various tipping points – it has reached the maturation of a particular vision of sustainability, emergency sustainability, that is linked to a balanced view of sustainable justice.

The examination of the ethical and critical aspects related to environmental law has also allowed us to better understand the aforementioned theories, such as the strong and weak approaches to sustainability, which are particularly reflected in the different natures of environmental law itself.

This work has also described a branch of studies and theoretical issues related to resilience that lends itself to different visions and interpretations. Resilience Law can be interpreted as a type of justice concerning vulnerability, rights, and forms of resistance, but it can also have other shades of meaning.

Through specific legal change theories, this branch finds its theoretical realisation through the pillar of equity, which stands as a corollary of resilience. "Resilient equity" looks to the future and uses law as a guarantor of universal well-being that is undermined by "disequity" regimes, which attempt to destroy the sustainable dynamics of civil life, both with regard to social relations and in the relationship between nature and man.

Resilience Law is a law that through the theoretical framework of "equity" – and therefore "equitable law" – attempts to pursue sustainable goals of resilience in an increasingly marked context from an emergency scenario. This scenario, in effect, involves different crises that extend over several levels and that range from the climate and earth crisis to the crisis of human and social values.

References

Allott, Philip. 1990. *Eunomia. New Order for a New World.* Oxford: Oxford University Press.

Allott, Philip. 1992. "Reconstituting Humanity - New International Law". *European Journal of International Law.*

Anguirre, Benigno E. 2007. "Dialectics of Vulnerability and Resilience". *Georgetown Journal on Poverty Law and Policy*, No. 14.

Arnaud, André-Jean. 1981. *Critique de la Raison Juridique. Où va la Sociologie du Droit?* Paris: LGDJ.

Atienza, Manuel. 2010. *Una Visión de la Filosofía del Derecho*. Facultad De Postgrado.

Attfield, Robin. 1981. "The Good of the Trees". *The Journal of Value Inquiry*, 15 (1): 35-54.

Baer, Paul, Kartha, Silvan, Athanasiou, Tom, and Kemp-Benedict, Eric. 2009. "The Greenhouse Development Rights Framework: Drawing Attention to Inequality within Nations in the Global Climate Policy Debate". *Development and Change*, 40.

Barnes, Richard A. 2013. "The Capacity of Property Rights to Accommodate Social Ecological Resilience". *Ecology & Society*, Vol. 18: 6.

Baslar, Kemal. 1998. *The Concept of the Common Heritage of Mankind in International Law.* Dordrecht, The Netherlands: Martinus Nijhoff Kluwer Law.

Benson, Melinda Harm. 2015. "Reconceptualizing Environmental Challenges: Is Resilience the New Narrative?". *Journal of Environmental and Sustainability Law*, Vol. 21.

Bentham, Jeremy. 2010. *Of the Limits of the Penal Branch of Jurisprudence*, Oxford: Oxford Univ. Press.

Berry, Thomas. 2002. "Rights of the Earth: We Need a New Legal Framework Which Recognises the Rights of All Living Beings". *Resurgence and Ecologist Magazine.*

Berry, Thomas. 1999. *The Great Work: Our Way into the Future.* New York: Harmony/Bell Tower.

Beyerlin, Ulrich. 2006. "Bridging the North-South Divide in International Environmental Law". *Zeitschrift für ausländisches öffentliches Recht und Völkerrecht*, No. 66.

Biber, Eric. 2017. "Law in the Anthropocene Epoch". *The Georgetown Law Journal*, Vol. 106: 1.

Birnie, Patricia, and Boyle, Alan. 1994. *International Law and the Environment*. Oxford: Oxford University Press.

Black Dog Institute. 2016. *Resilience@Law. Legal Profession, Mental Health Toolkit. Practical Guide & Resources*. Randwick.

Bobbio, Norberto. 1990. *L'età dei diritti*, Torino: Einaudi.

Bobbio, Norberto. 2014. *Elogio della mitezza*. Milano: Il Saggiatore.

Bosselmann, Klaus. 2002. "The Concept of Sustainable Development". In *Environmental Law for a Sustainable Society*, edited by Klaus Bosselmann and David Grinlinton. Auckland, N.Z.: New Zealand Centre for Environmental Law.

Bosselmann, Klaus. 2006. "Strong and Weak Sustainable Development: Making Differences in The Design of Law". *South African Journal of Environmental Law and Policy*, No. 13.

Bosselmann, Klaus. 2008. *The Principle of Sustainability: Transforming Law and Governance*. Farnham: Ashgate.

Bosselmann, Klaus. 2010. "Losing the Forest for the Trees: Environmental Reductionism in the Law". *Sustainability*, No. 2.

Bosselmann, Klaus. 2016. "A Normative Approach to Environmental Governance: Sustainability at the Apex of Environmental Law". In *Research Handbook on Fundamental Concepts of Environmental Law*, edited by Douglas Fisher. Cheltenham: Edward Elgar.

Bosselmann, Klaus. 2017. *The Principle of Sustainability: Transforming Law and Governance*, 2nd ed. Abingdon and New York: Routledge.

Bosselmann, Klaus. 2020. "Sustainable Development Law". In *Routledge Handbook of International Environmental Law*, edited by Erika Techera, Jade Lindley, Karen N. Scott, and Anastasia Telesetsky. Routledge.

Bougen, Philip D. 2003. "Catastrophe Risk". *Economy and Society*, no. 32 (2): 253–274.

Bouyé, Mathilde, Harmeling, Sven, and Schulz, Nils-Sjard. 2018. *Connecting the Dots: Elements for a Joined-Up Implementation of the 2030 Agenda and Paris Agreement*. Washington: World Resources Institute.

Boyle, Alan. 1999. "Codification of International Environmental Law and the International Law Commission: Injurious Consequences Revisited". In *International Law and Sustainable Development*, edited by Alan Boyle and David Freestone. Oxford: Oxford University Press.

Brand, Fridolin Simon, and Jax, Kurt. 2007. "Focusing the meaning of resilience: resilience as a descriptive concept and a boundary object". *Ecology and Society*, 12 (1).

Brown Donald & Taylor Prue. 2014. "Ethics and Climate Change. A Study of National Commitments", IUCN *Environmental Policy and Law Paper*, no. 86.

Brown, Donald A. 2013. *White Paper on the Ethical Dimensions of Climate Change*. Widener Law School Legal Studies Research Paper.

Brown Weiss, Edith. 1992. "Intergenerational equity: a legal framework for global environmental change". In *Environmental Change and International Law*: *New Challenges and Dimensions*, edited by Edith Brown Weiss. Tokyo: United Nations University Press.

Brown Weiss, Edith. 1993. "Intergenerational Equity: Toward an International Legal Framework". *Global Accord: Environmental Challenges and International Responses*. Cambridge.

Burdon, Peter. 2011. *Exploring Wild Law: The Philosophy of Earth Jurisprudence*. Kent Town, South Australia: Wakefield Press.

Burdon, Peter. 2014. "Wild Law and the Project of Earth Democracy". In *Wild Law - in Practice*, edited by Michelle Maloney and Peter Burdon. London: Routledge.

Busch, Per-Olof, and Jorgens, Helge. 2012. "Governance by Diffusion: Exploring a New Mechanism of International Policy Coordination". In *Governance, Democracy and Sustainable Development*: *Moving Beyond the Impasse?* Edited by James Meadowcroft, Oluf Langhelle, and Audun Ruud. Cheltenham and Northampton, MA: Edward Elgar.

Caney, Simon. 2005. "Cosmopolitan Justice, Responsibility, and Global Climate Change". *Leiden Journal of International Law*, Vol. 18.

Caney, Simon. 2009. "Justice and the Distribution of Greenhouse Gas Emissions". *Journal of Global Ethics*, Vol. 5.

Ciaramelli, Fabio. 2018. "La vulnerabilità: da caratteristica dei soggetti a carattere del diritto". In *Vulnerabilità. Analisi multidisciplinare di un concetto*, edited by Orsetta Giolo and Baldassarre Pastore. Roma: Carocci.

Cordonier Segger, Marie-Claire and Khalfan, Ashfaq. 2004. *Sustainable Development Law. Principles, Practices and Prospects*. Oxford: Oxford University Press.

Cordonier Segger, Marie-Claire, and Weeramantry, Christopher. 2017. *Sustainable Development Principles in the Decisions of International Courts and Tribunals*: 1992-2012. London: Routledge Ltd.

Cosens, Barbara. 2012. "Resilience and Law as a Theoretical Backdrop for Natural Resource Management: Flood Management in the Columbia River Basin". *Environmental Law*, 42.

Craig, Robin Kundis. 2013. "Learning to Think About Complex Environmental Systems in Environmental and Natural Resource Law and Legal Scholarship: A Twenty-Year Retrospective". *Fordham Environmental Law Review*, no. 24.

Cullinan, Cormac. 2002. *Wild Law. A Manifesto for Earth Justice*. London: Chelsea Green Pub Co.

De Sousa Santos, Boaventura. 1987. "Law: A Map of Misreading. Toward a Postmodern Conception of Law". *Journal of Law & Society*, 14.

De Sousa Santos, Boaventura. 1995. *Toward a New Common Sense. Law, Science and Politics in the Paradigmatic Transition*. New York: Routledge.

Demange, Lia Helena Monteiro de Lima. 2013. "The Principle of Resilience". *Pace Environmental Law Review,* vol. 30, issue 2, 695.

Dernbach, John C. 2002. "Sustainable Development: Now More than Ever". *Environmental Law Reporter*, vol. 32, no. 1.

Dobson, Andrew. 1996. "Environmental Sustainability: An Analysis and Typology". *Environmental Politics*, 5.

Douglas, William Oriville. 1972. "Mr. Justice Douglas, Dissenting", *Living Wilderness*, no. 36.

Durkheim, Emile. 1893. *De la Division du Travail Social*. Paris.

Duus-Otterström, Göran, and C. Jagers, Sverker. 2011. "Why (most) climate insurance schemes are a bad idea". *Environmental Politics*, no. 20 (3).

Ehrlich, Eugen. 1936. *Fundamental Principles of Sociology of Law*. Translated by Walter Lewis Moll. Cambridge, MA: Harvard University Press.

Elwell, Frank W. 2013. *Sociocultural Systems. Principles of Structure and Change*. Edmonton: Au Press, Athabasca University.

Febbrajo, Alberto. 2013. "Limiti della regolazione giuridica nelle crisi intersistemiche". C*risi Economica e Trasformazioni della dimensione giuridica*, edited by Raffaele Bifulco and Orlando Roselli. Torino: G. Giappichelli.

Fischman, Robert L. 2019. "Letting Go of Stability: Resilience and Environmental Law". *Indiana Law Journal. Indiana Legal Studies Research Paper*, no. 397.

Fisher, Douglas. 2013. *Legal Reasoning in Environmental Law: A Study of Structure, Form and Language.* Cheltenham: Edward Elgar.

Frank, Jerome. 1930. *Law and the Modern Mind*. New York: Tudor Pub. Com.

Friedman, Lawrence M. 1975. *The Legal System. A Social Science Perspective*. New York: Russell Sage Foundation.

Gardiner, Stephen. 2006. "A core precautionary principle". *Journal of Political Philosophy*, no. 14 (1): 33-60.

Garmestani, Ahjond S., Allen, Craig R., and Cabezas, Heriberto. 2009. "Panarchy, Adaptive Management and Governance: Policy Options for Building Resilience". *Nebraska Law Review*, No. 87.

Garmestani, Ahjond S., Allen, Craig R., Arnold, Craig Anthony, and Gunderson, Lance H. 2014. *Social-Ecological Resilience and Law*. New York: Columbia University Press, No. 142.

Gaudemet, Jean. 1976. "Les Transfert de Droit". *L'Année Sociologique*, 29.

Georgescu-Roegen, Nicholas. 1986. "The entropy law and the economic process in retrospect". *Eastern Economic Journal*, no. 12: 3-25.

Giddens, Anthony. 1990. *The Consequences of Modernity*. Cambridge: Polity Press.

Gillespie, Alexander. 1997. *International Environmental Law, Policy and Ethics*. Oxford: Clarendon Press Oxford.

Gillroy, John Martin. 2006. "Adjudication Norms, Dispute Settlement Regimes and International Tribunals: The Status of Environmental Sustainability in International Jurisprudence". *Stanford Journal of International Law.* No. 42: 1.

Gogoi, Elizabeth, Bahadur, Aditya V, and Rumbaitis del Rio, Cristina. 2017. "Mainstreaming Adaptation to Climate Change within Governance Systems in South Asia: An Analytical Framework and Examples from Practice". *Learning Paper*. New Delhi: Action on Climate Today.

Gosseries, Axel. 2008. "Lo scetticismo sui diritti delle generazioni future è giustificato?". In *Un diritto per il futuro. Teorie e modelli dello sviluppo sostenibile e della responsabilità intergenerazionale*, edited by Raffaele Bifulco and Antonio D'Aloia. Napoli.

Grasso, Marco Ettore. 2012. *Il mutamento climatico e il diritto alla salute*. Milano: Franco Angeli.

Grasso, Marco Ettore. 2015. *Lineamenti di Etica e Diritto della Sostenibilità*, Centro di Studi sulla Giustizia. Milano: Giuffrè.

Grasso, Marco Ettore. 2017. "Natural Catastrophes and Forms of Catastrophism. A New Ethical and Moral Framework Leading Towards the Responsible Catastrophism Model". In *The Role of Integrity in the Governance of the Commons: Governance, Ecology, Law, Ethics*, edited by Laura Westra, Janice Gray and Franz-Theo Gottwald. Cham: Springer.

Grasso, Marco Ettore. 2019. "Emergency Sustainability and Ethics: Climate Change, Epistemic Health and Nihilism". In *Ecological Integrity and Land Uses: Sovereignty, Governance, Displacements and Land Grabs*, edited by Laura Westra, Klaus Bosselmann and Virginia Zambrano. New York: Nova Science Pub.

Grear, Anna. 2013. "Law's Entities: Complexity, Plasticity and Justice". *Jurisprudence*, no. 4, 1.

Greenhalgh, Trisha. 2004. "Meta-Narrative Mapping: A New Approach to the Synthesis of Complex Evidence". In *Narrative Research in Health and Illness*, edited by Brian Hurwitz, Trisha Greenhalgh, and Vieda Skultans. Blackwell Pub.

Grove, Kevin, and Chandler, David. 2017. "Introduction: Resilience and the Anthropocene: The Stakes of 'Renaturalising' Politics". *Resilience*, vol. 5, no. 2.

Hart, Herbert Lionel Adolphus. 1961. *The Concept of Law*. Oxford: Oxford University Press.

Holling, Crawford Stanley. 1973. "Resilience and Stability of Ecological Systems". *Annual Review of Ecology and Systematics*, vol. 4: 1-23.

Hudson, Paul, Botzen, Wouter, Czajkowski, Jeffrey, and Kreibich, Heidi. 2017. "Moral hazard in natural disaster insurance markets: Empirical evidence from Germany and the United States". *Land Economics*, no. 93 (2).

Humby, Tracy-Lynn. 2014. "Law and Resilience: Mapping the Literature". *Seattle Journal of Environmental Law*, vol. 4: iss. 1, article 4.

Hunter, David, Salzman, James, and Zaelke, Durwood. 2001. *International Environmental Law and Policy*. New York: Foundation Press.

Jessup C., Philip. 1956. *Transnational Law*. New Haven: Yale University Press.

Joseph, Jonathan. 2016. "Governing Through Failure and Denial: The New Resilience Agenda". *Millennium*: *Journal of International Studies*, Vol. 44, Issue 3.

Kelsen, Hans. 1967. *Pure Theory of Law*. Translated by Max Knight. Berkeley, CA: University of California Press.

Kim, Rakhyun, and Bosselmann, Klaus. 2013. "International Environmental Law in the Anthropocene: Towards a Purposive System of Multilateral Environmental Agreements". *Transnational Environmental Law*, no. 2, 2.

Kiss, Alexandre Charles, and Shelton, Dinah. 1994. *International Environmental Law*. New York. Transnational Publishers.

Koddenbrock, Kai. 2015. "Strategies of Critique in International Relatios: From Foucault and Latour Towards Marx". *European Journal of International Relations*, 21, no. 2.

Kornélia, Horváth Luca. 2012. "A Preliminary Examination of the Possibilities for the Institutional Representation of the Interest of Future Generations and Environmental Protection within the System of the United Nations". In *Stakeholder Forum's Programme on Sustainable Development Governance*. Office for the Hungarian Parliamentary Commissioner.

Kotzé, Louis J. 2019. "Earth System Law for the Anthropocene". *Sustainability*, 11, 6796.
Kotzé, Louis J., Kim, Rakhyun E. 2019. "Earth System Law: The Juridical Dimensions of Earth System Governance". *Earth System Governance*, 1.
Lenski, Gerhard. 2005. "Ecological-Evolutionary Theory: Principles and Applications". *Canadian Journal of Sociology Online*, September-October.
Lowe, Alan Vaughan. 1999. "Sustainable Development and Unsustainable Arguments". In *International Law and Sustainable Development. Past Achievements and Future Challenges*, edited by Alan Boyle and David Freestone. Oxford: Oxford University Press.
Luhmann, Niklas. 1964. "Funktionale Methode und Systemtheorie". *Soziale Welt*, No. 15: 1-25.
Luhmann, Niklas. 1981. *Ausdifferenzierung des Rechts, Beiträge zur Rechtssoziologie und Rechtstheorie*. Frankfurt/Main: Fundstellen im Portalbestand.
Luhmann, Niklas. 1984. *Soziale Systeme. Grundriß einer allgemeinen Theorie*. Frankfurt: Suhrkamp.
Luhmann, Niklas. 1993. *Das Recht der Gesellschaft*. Frankfurt: Suhrkamp.
Maine, Henry. 1861. *Ancient Law*. London.
Malm, Andreas, and Hornborg, Alf. 2014. "The Geology of Mankind? A Critique of the Anthropocene Narrative". *The Anthropocene Review*, 1, 1.
Maloney, Michelle, and Siemen, Sister Patricia. 2015. "Responding to the Great Work: the Role of Earth Jurisprudence and Wild Law in the 21st Century". *Environmental and Earth Law Journal*, no. 5, 1.
Marie-Claire Cordonier Segger and Christopher Weeramantry. 2005. *Sustainable Justice: Reconciling Economic, Social and Environmental Law*. Leiden, The Netherlands: Koninklijke Brill.
Maruotti, Laura Solidoro. 2012. "Aequitas e Ius Scriptum. Profili Storici". *Annali della Facoltà Giuridica dell'Università di Camerino – n. 1/2012.*
Miller, David. 2008. *Global Justice and Climate Change: How Should Responsibilities Be Distributed?* Beijing: Tsinghua University.
Moellendorf, Darrell. 2009. *Global Inequality Matters*. New York.
Morand Deviller, Jacqueline, and Bénichot, Jean-Claude. 2010. *Mondialisation et Globalization des Concepts Juridiques: L'Exxemple du Droit de l'Environnement*. IRJS.
Morin, Edgar. 1990. *Introduction à la Pensée Complexe*. Paris: ESF.
Nash, Roderick F. 1989. *The Rights of Nature: A History of Environmental Ethics*. Madison, Wisconsin: The University of Wisconsin Press.
Norton, Bryan G. 1982. "Environmental Ethics and Nonhuman Rights". *Environmental Ethics*, vol. 4.

Norton, Bryan G. 1984. "Environmental Ethics and Weak Anthropocentrism". *Environmental Ethics*, no. 6, 2.

O'Hare, Paul, White, Iain, and Connelly, Angela. 2015. "Insurance as maladaptation: Resilience and the 'business as usual' paradox". *Environment and Planning C: Government and Policy*, no. 34 (6).

O'Neill, Onora. 1996. *Towards Justice and Virtue: A Constructive Account of Practical Reasoning*. Cambridge: Cambridge University Press.

Ost, François, and Van De Kerchove, Michel. 2002. *De la Pyramide au Réseau? Pour une Théorie Dialectique du Droit*. Bruxelles: Publications des Facultés universitaires Saint-Louis.

Passerin d'Entrèves, Alessandro. 2018. *Obbedienza e resistenza. Le leggi vanno sempre rispettate?* Edizioni di Comunità.

Passmore, John. 1980. *Man's Responsibility for Nature. Ecological Problems and Western Traditions*. London: Duckworth.

Philippopoulos-Mihalopoulos, Andreas. 2011. *Law and Ecology: New Environmental Foundations*. London: Routledge.

Philippopoulos-Mihalopoulos, Andreas. 2013. "Actors or Spectators? Vulnerability and Critical Environmental Law". *Oñati Socio-Legal Series*, No 3, 5.

Podgórecki, Adam. 1996. "Sociotechnics: Basic Concepts and Issues". In *Social Engineering*, edited by Adam Podgôrecki, Jon Alexander and Rob Shields. Ottawa.

Posner, Eric, and Weisbach, David. 2010. *Climate Change Justice*. Princeton: Princeton University Press.

Pound, Roscoe. 1938. *The Formative Era of American Law*. Little, Brown & Company.

Preston, Brian J. 2016. "The Judicial Development of Ecologically Sustainable Development". In *Research Handbook on Fundamental Concepts of Environmental Law*, edited by Douglas Fisher. Cheltenham: Edward Elgar.

Rawls, John. 1999. *The Law of Peoples*. Cambridge, Massachusetts: Harvard University Press.

Regan, Tom. 1983. *The Case for Animal Rights*. Berkeley and Los Angeles: University of California Press.

Rescher, Nicholas. 1983. "Unpopular Essays on Technological Progress". *The Philosophical Review*, vol. 92, no. 3. Duke University Press.

Robinson, Nicholas A. 2014. Fundamental Principles of Law for the Anthropocene? *Environmental Policy and Law*, 44/1-2. Pace Law Faculty Publications.

Rodière, René. 1978. *Approche d'un Phénomène: Les Migrations de Systèmes Juridiques*. Tolouse: Université des sciences sociales de Toulouse, 947.

Rouland, Norbert. 1988. *Antropologie Juridique*. Paris.

Ruhl, J. B. 1997. "Thinking of Environmental Law as a Complex Adaptive System: How to Clean up the Environment by Making a Mess of Environmental Law". *Houston Law Review*, 34.

Ruhl, J. B. 2010. "General Design Principles for Resilience and Adaptive Capacity in Legal Systems – With applications to Climate Change Adaptation and Resiliency in Legal Systems". *North Carolina Law Review*, no. 89.

Runhaar, Hens, Wilk, Bettina, Persson, Asa, Uittenbroek, Caroline, Wamsler, Christine. 2017. "Mainstreaming Climate Adaptation: Taking Stock about 'What Works' from Empirical Research Worldwide". *Regional Environmental Change*; no. 18 (4).

Sands, Philippe. 1994. "International Law in the Field of Sustainable Development". *British Yearbook of International Law*, vol. 65, no. 1.

Sands, Philippe. 1995. *Principles of International Environmental Law.* Manchester and New York: Manchester Univ. Press.

Sands, Philippe. 2003. *Principles of International Environmental Law*, 2nd ed. Cambridge: Cambridge Univ. Press.

Sari, Aurel 2019. "Legal Resilience in an Era of Gray Zone Conflicts and Hybrid Threats". *Working Papers Series 2019/1*. Exeter Centre for International Law.

Schauer, Frederick. 2000. "The Politics and Incentives of Legal Transplantation". In *Governance in a Globalizing World*, edited by Joseph S. Nye and John D. Donahue. Cambridge, 253.

Schauer, Frederick. 2013. "The Jurisprudence of Custom". *Texas International Law Journal*, vol. 48: 523-534.

Schmidt, Jessica. 2014. "Intuitively Neoliberal? Towards a Critical Understanding of Resilience Governance". *European Journal of International Relations*.

Schrijver, Nico. 2005. "The New Delhi Declaration of Principles of International Law Relating to Sustainable Development". In *Sustainable Justice: Reconciling Economic, Social and Environmental Law*, edited by Marie-Claire Cordonier Segger and Christopher Weeramantry. Leiden, The Netherlands: Koninklijke Brill.

Selznick, Philip, and Nonet, Philippe. 1978. *Law and Society in Transition: Toward Responsive Law*. New York.

Shapiro, Martin. 1993. "The Globalization of Law". *Indiana Journal of Global Legal Studies*, 1, 37.

Slovic, Paul, Fischhoff, Baruch, and Lichtenstein, Sarah. 1977. "Behavioral decision theory". *Annual Review of Psychology*, No. 28: 1-39.

Stone, Christopher. 1974. *Should Trees Have Standing? Toward legal rights for natural objects*. Los Altos: California: William Kaufman.

Taleb, Nassim Nicholas. 2012. *Things that gain from disorder*. London: Penguin.

Tamanaha, Brian Z. 2001. *A General Jurisprudence of Law and Society*. Oxford.

Taylor, Paul W. 1986. *Respect For Nature. A Theory of Environmental Ethics*. Princeton: Princeton University Press.

Teubner, Günther. 1997. "Global Bukowina: Legal Pluralism in the World Society". In *Global Law Without a State*, edited by Günther Teubner. Dartmouth: Aldershot.

Tews, Kerstin. 2011. "The Diffusion of Environmental Policy Innovations". In *Multilevel Governance of Global Environmental Change: Perspectives from Science, Sociology and the Law*, edited by Gerd Winter. Cambridge, New York: Cambridge University Press: 227-252.

Thoreau, Henry David. 1849. *Resistance to Civil Government*. Æsthetic Papers, edited by Elizabeth P. Peabody. Boston and New York: The Editor and G. P. Putnam.

Tol, Richard S. J. 1998. "Climate change and insurance: a critical appraisal". *Energy Policy*, Vol. 26, No. 3: 257-262.

Traxler, Martino. 2002. "Fair Chore Division for Climate Change". *Social Theory and Practice*, Vol. 28, 1.

Twining, William. 2000. *Globalization and Legal Theory*. London: Butterworths.

Twining, William. 2009. *General Jurisprudence. Understanding Law from a Global Perspective*. Cambridge: Cambridge University Press.

Voigt, Christina. 2009. *Sustainable Development as a Principle of International Law. Resolving Conflicts between Climate Measures and WTO Law*. Leiden-Boston: Martinus Nijhoff Publishers.

Wallis, Steven E., and Valentinov, Vladislav. 2016. "What is Sustainable Theory? A Luhmannian Perspective on the Science of Conceptual Systems". *Foundations of Science*, No. 22 (4).

Ward, Halina. 2009. "Learning from the Hungarian Parliamentary Commissioner for Future Generations". *UKELA E-Law*.

Watson, Alan. 1974. *Legal Transplants: An Approach to Comparative Law*. University Press of Virginia.

Watson, Alan. 1976. "Legal Transplant and Law Reform". *Law Quarterly Review*, 92.

Watson, Alan. 1977. *Society and Legal Change*, Edinburgh.

Watson, Alan. 1984. *Sources of Law, Legal Change and Ambiguity*. Philadelphia.

Watson, Alan. 1985. *The Evolution of Law*. Baltimore.
Watson, Alan. 1996. *Aspects of Reception of Law*. Scholarly Works.
Watson, Richard A. 1979. "Self-Consciousness and the Rights of Non human Animals and Nature". *Environmental Ethics*, 1: 99-129.
Weber, Max. 1922. *Wirtschaft und Gesellschaft*. Tübingen.
Westra, Laura. 1998. *Living in Integrity. A Global Ethic to Restore a Fragmented Earth*. Rowman & Littlefield Pub Inc.
Westra, Laura. 2006. *Environmental Justice and the Rights of Unborn and Future Generations: Law, Environmental Harm and the Right to Health*. London: Earthscan, Routledge.
Westra, Laura, Juss, Satvinder and Scovazzi, Tullio. 2015. *Towards a Refugee Oriented Right of Asylum*. Farnham, Surrey: Ashgate, Publishing Ltd.
Westra, Laura. 2016. *Ecological Integrity and Global Governance. Science, Ethics and the Law*. Routledge.
Westra, Laura. 2021. *Forced Migrations and Refugees in the Mediterranean Basin and the MENA Region*. New York: Nova Science Publishers, Inc.
Wilkinson, David. 2002. *Environment and Law*. London: Routledge.
Wise, Edward M. 1990. "The Transplant of Legal Patterns". *The American Journal of Comparative Law*, 38.
Wood, Stepan, and Ellis, Jaye. 2006. "International Environmental Law". In *Environmental Law for Sustainability*, edited by Benjamin J. Richardson, and Stepan Wood. Oxford, UK: Hart Publishing.
Worrell, Richard, and Appleby, Michael. 1999. "Stewardship of Natural Resources: Definition, Ethical and Practical Aspects". *Journal of Agricultural & Environmental Ethics*, No. 12, 3.
Yang, Tseming, and Percival, Robert V. 2009. "The Emergence of Global Environmental Law". *Ecology Law Quarterly*, 36 (3).
Zumbansen, Peer. 2008. "Transnational Law". *Comparative Research in Law & Political Economy*, vol. 04, no. 02.
Zumbansen, Peer. 2014. "What Lies Before, Behind and Beneath a Case? Five Minutes of Transnational Lawyering and the Consequences for Legal Education". In *Stateless Law: Evolving Boundaries of a Discipline*, edited by Helge Dedek and Shauna Van Praagh. Ashgate.
Zumbansen, Peer. 2015. "Theorizing as Activity: Transnational Legal Theory in Context". *TLI Think! Research Paper*, 04/2015: 5.